FINANCE

An International Perspective

Irwin Perspectives in International Business

Series Coeditors
James E. Harf *The Ohio State University*
Robert R. Miller *University of Houston*
B. Thomas Trout *University of New Hampshire*

FINANCE

An International Perspective

Arthur I. Stonehill
Oregon State University

David K. Eiteman
University of California—Los Angeles

1987

Homewood, Illinois 60430

© RICHARD D. IRWIN, INC., 1987

ISBN 0-256-05629-3

Library of Congress Catalog Card No. 86–81805

Printed in the United States of America

2 3 4 5 6 7 8 9 0 K 4 3 2 1 0 9 8 7

To our wives, Kari and Keng-Fong

PREFACE

Finance: An International Perspective is one of a series of six volumes produced under the direction of the Consortium for International Studies Education with support from the U.S. Department of Education. The specific aim of the series is to provide an international dimension for the core functional courses in business administration for colleges and universities. The first four volumes are intended to be used in conjunction with introductory textbooks in accounting, finance, management, and marketing. The other two books provide supplemental material for the introduction to business course; the first discusses international environmental matters, while the second addresses managerial issues. Books in the series have been tailored to supplement individual chapters in many of the leading textbooks in the core areas covered.

Each volume was produced under the general direction of a team leader. In most cases this leader also coauthored the respective area book. Team leaders were:

Accounting:	Professor Gerhard G. Mueller, University of Washington
Finance:	Professor Arthur I. Stonehill, Oregon State University
Management:	Professor R. Hal Mason, University of California, Los Angeles
Marketing:	Professor Philip Cateora, University of Colorado
Introduction to Business:	Professor Robert R. Miller, University of Houston–University Park

Each of these leaders has authored or coauthored leading international textbooks in their areas of scholarly expertise. Each has also produced numerous technical articles. Volumes in this series and their authors are:

Accounting: An International Perspective, by Gerhard G. Mueller, Helen Gernon (University of Oregon), and Gary Meek (Oklahoma State University).

Finance: An International Perspective, by Arthur I. Stonehill and David K. Eiteman (UCLA).

Management: An International Perspective, by R. Hal Mason and Robert Spich (UCLA).

Marketing: An International Perspective, by Philip Cateora and Susan Keaveney (University of Colorado).

Introduction to Business: An International Perspective, by Janice J. Miller (University of Houston) and Robert R. Miller.

Issues for Managers: An International Perspective, by John A. Kilpatrick (University of Northern Colorado) and Janice J. Miller.

Codirectors of the project for the Consortium were James E. Harf (The Ohio State University), B. Thomas Trout (University of New Hampshire), and Robert R. Miller.

Department of Education sponsorship of this project was a part of its efforts to expand international awareness in U.S. higher education. In this regard, the Department's interests coincided with those of the American Assembly of Collegiate Schools of Business (AACSB), which recently included internationalization of curricula as a requirement for accreditation of American college and university degree programs in business administration. This emphasis by AACSB is likely to be strengthened in coming years, and the series of which this volume is a part is dedicated specifically to satisfying the AACSB mandate.

Finance: An International Perspective was written to provide beginning business finance students with an awareness of the applicability and limitations of business finance theories and practices when applied to the financial management of international business.

Most introductory business finance texts position an international chapter at or toward the end of the book, implying possibly that "international" is something separate from the main body of finance, as well as risking the possibility that the international aspects of business finance will be ignored in the rush at the end of the term. We believe that international material can more readily be absorbed if integrated with domestic financial management as it is treated in a basic text. This belief arises from the observation that most basic financial management problems exist in both domestic and international versions, but sometimes a flexible perspective is needed to handle international complexities.

The single international topic with no domestic counterpart is foreign exchange rates. For that reason, chapters on this material must be assigned early in an introductory course so that additional topics can be viewed in their worldwide context when they are first introduced. Other than the topic of foreign exchange, international material should be introduced simultaneously with financial topics in the regular introductory text. A classification is provided at the end of this preface that relates each chapter in this small international finance book to the relevant chapters in several of the major business finance texts.

Finance: An International Perspective is intended for junior level undergraduate students who have completed an introductory accounting course and who have taken an elementary economics course. The book is also appropriate as parallel material for core courses in MBA curriculums, and it can easily be integrated into seminars for executives who wish to know more about international finance without having to read a full-length text on that subject.

It took approximately two years to plan and write this book, and another half year to have it tested in finance classes at the University of Hawaii at Manoa. Valuable suggestions from Professor Russell Taussig of the University of Hawaii and his students have been incorporated, and the authors are very appreciative. As most readers will be aware, the present value of such suggestions, received at time zero (before publication) is much greater than if they were to become apparent only after students had begun struggling with the final printed word. Nevertheless, the authors remain responsible for errors and confusion. They would welcome any suggestions for future editions, either in the form of comments on material covered in this first edition or on other material which might have been included.

Arthur I. Stonehill
Corvallis, Oregon

David K. Eiteman
Pacific Palisades, California

CONTENTS

The International Dimensions of Finance

What is so unique about international finance that it requires special attention in a corporate finance course as well as in business practice?

Four factors make international finance unique. They are:

1. A different socio-political environment.
2. The presence of foreign exchange risk.
3. Taxation by more than one government.
4. Unique institutional factors.

Chapter One describes how socio-political factors constrain the selection of corporate financial goals for foreign operations. Chapter Two describes how foreign exchange rates are quoted, how the foreign exchange market functions, and how one forecasts foreign exchange rate changes. Chapter Three analyzes how a firm manages its foreign exchange risk. Chapter Four analyzes how political, tax, and institutional factors impact the management of a firm's working capital. Chapter Five describes the main institutional factors that enable a firm to expand its sources of capital, including the Eurocurrency market, the Eurobond market, and trade financing instruments. Chapter Six analyzes how a firm can lower its cost of capital through international sourcing of its funds. Chapter Seven illustrates by example how international complications can be incorporated into the capital budgeting analysis of a foreign project.

FINANCIAL GOALS IN THEORY

According to current finance theory, the goal of the firm should be to maximize the shareholders' wealth. This is achieved by maximizing the present value of future dividends and capital gains on the firm's common stock. The market value of the firm's stock is deemed to be a function of its rate of return and risk in a portfolio context since the typical shareholder is assumed to hold a well-diversified portfolio of securities. Financial executives are expected to follow this objective when choosing which long-term projects to pursue, how to finance these projects, how to manage working capital, and what proportion of earnings to pay out as dividends.

When a firm expands its operations to foreign locations, operating decisions designed to maximize its home-country shareholders' wealth almost invariably collide with cultural, institutional, and political constraints imposed by the foreign environment. For example, a host-country government typically pursues national economic, social, and political goals that constrain the activities of both foreign and domestic firms operating within that country. These goals sometimes act against the best interests of the foreign firm's shareholders.

Multinational firms sometimes operate joint ventures with local partners in the host country. Such partners are only interested in the return and risk of the joint venture itself. They are not concerned about the return and risk of the joint venture from the perspective of the well-diversified shareholders of the multinational firm, nor are they concerned with how the local joint venture fits into the worldwide strategy of the multinational parent.

A multinational firm typically staffs its foreign operations almost entirely with host-country nationals. Their cultural norms, experiences, and loyalties are attuned to the local environment. It is difficult for them to relate to a goal of maximizing the wealth of distant shareholders, who hold shares whose price is determined by little-understood variables interacting on a foreign stock exchange.

HOST-COUNTRY PUBLIC POLICY CONSTRAINTS

Public policy constraints imposed by host governments may conflict with the goal of maximizing the wealth of a multinational firm's shareholders. These include economic constraints imposed on foreign subsidiaries by host-country monetary, fiscal, balance of payments, and economic development policies. In addition, foreign-owned firms face political risks caused by possible changes in the host country's government or changes in its policy toward foreign-owned firms.

Monetary Policy

Most countries attempt to influence economic growth, employment, inflation, and their balance of payments by controlling the cost and availability of funds. In some cases, subsidiaries of multinational firms appear immune to host-country monetary policy. If local credit is rationed, for example, local competitors with access only to the host country's money and capital markets must postpone expansion plans and live with expensive and scarce credit. Foreign subsidiaries of multinational firms located in that country, however, have access to funds outside the control of the host government. They can borrow from the parent firm, sister subsidiaries, or even international markets. Host-country monetary policy does not necessarily curb their ability to expand; and, in fact, they may be given a competitive advantage over their local competitors. Of course, host governments have other instruments that might be used to curtail this expansion, but at least the foreign government's monetary policy can be frustrated.

Fiscal Policy

In an effort to attract foreign investment, host governments sometimes grant "tax holidays" whereby taxes are forgiven for the first few years of the investment. Once the foreign subsidiary is established, however, the host government may regret such a tax concession. Presence of a successful and expanding foreign firm may create the need for the government to provide social overhead for the investment (such as roads, schools, hospitals, and housing) even when the firm does not yet provide a tax base to finance these services.

Even without concessions, host countries suspect that at times multinational firms are able to reduce their local taxable income by manipulating "transfer prices," which are sales or purchases of goods and services to related subsidiaries or the parent. In fact, this very problem has motivated a number of states in the United States to assess a "unitary tax" when taxing foreign subsidiaries within their jurisdiction. The unitary tax is based on the worldwide income of the multinational firm rather than on the income reported as earned in the state. For example, if the California subsidiary of Toyota Motors represents 10 percent of Toyota's worldwide employment, assets, and sales, then 10 percent of Toyota's worldwide income is assumed to be earned in California and is so taxed. Transfer pricing is discussed in more detail in Chapter Four.

Balance of Payments Policy

Governments are sometimes forced to follow restrictive policies designed to cure a balance of payments deficit or to support the foreign exchange value of their currency. Most of these policies affect foreign and domestic firms alike; but one such policy—blocking the transfer of funds into other currencies—is particularly damaging to foreign-owned firms. A foreign subsidiary may be earning a profit in the host country, but if these profits cannot be remitted to the parent because they are blocked, they may be of little value to the parent firm's shareholders. For example, what use are cruzados earned by a U.S. subsidiary in Brazil if cruzados cannot be converted into dollars? The cruzados cannot be used to pay dividends to shareholders, to repay dollar debt of the parent firm, or to expand the worldwide operations of the firm outside of Brazil.

Economic Development Policy

Although many nations court foreign direct investment in order to stimulate economic development, they also sometimes impose limitations that are not always in the best interests of the foreign firm's shareholders. India, Mexico, Brazil, Argentina, and many developing countries, for example, expect the multinational firm to obtain from the local economy an increasing proportion of their components, supplies, management, and other inputs. Although this may be reasonable from the perspective of enhancing economic development of the host country, it may interfere with the most efficient and cost-effective means of production, given the multinational firm's access to worldwide sources. As a result, goods produced with a high local content may be too costly to compete with imports unless they are protected by tariffs. In that case, the local population pays a higher price for goods than would be the case without interference in the sourcing decision.

Economic development policy sometimes requires a foreign firm to accept local ownership of a portion of the equity of their subsidiary. Such a joint venture might prove useful if the local partner or investors contribute their share of total financing, technology, and management, as well as pay a fair price for their share of the equity. Even if this occurs, however, many potential conflicts of interest could be detrimental to the shareholders of the multinational firm. For example, conflicts can arise over the subsidiary's dividend policy; transfer pricing on goods purchased from, or sold to, related firms; exports to unrelated firms previously served by one of the joint venture partners; the degree of local sourcing; the location of research and development; and the degree of disclosure necessary to satisfy local shareholders. Indeed, these problems were so serious that IBM withdrew its operations from India in 1977 when the Indian government insisted on some degree of local ownership of the subsidiary.

Political Risk

The most dramatic examples of public policy constraints occur as a result of political unrest or change in the host country. Few firms would establish a subsidiary in a country expecting an imminent revolution or a change to some radical form of government. Nevertheless, political conditions have a habit of changing after the direct foreign investment has been made. Multinational firms that invested in Cuba when Battista was the dictator never expected the extreme shift from a right-wing government to a communist government under Fidel Castro. Few firms expected the deposed Shah of Iran to be succeeded by a religious fanatic. In both cases, the results for foreign-owned firms and their shareholders were disastrous.

Expropriations (takeovers) of foreign subsidiaries by the governments of Cuba and Iran are extreme examples of political risk. Nevertheless, many examples exist where host countries have created misery for foreign-owned firms without actually expropriating them. Foreign-owned firms can suffer discriminatory taxation, overzealous application of health and environmental regulations, inability to release unneeded workers in order to cut costs, government-sponsored labor unrest and consumer boycotts, and numerous other forms of interference that make it impossible for the firm to operate profitably.

There have been times when foreign-owned firms were held hostage by the host government because it had poor relations with the parent firm's country. Foreign-owned firms in Libya in 1986 were in just such a predicament.

COMPARATIVE FINANCIAL GOALS

Shareholder wealth maximization is not universally accepted in practice as the unquestioned financial goal of the firm. In fact, it wasn't even the accepted goal in the theoretical finance literature in the United States until the late 1950s.[1] Prior to that time, the financial goal of the firm was assumed to be profit maximization. In practice, this meant maximizing earnings per share or maximizing net present value when related to a capital budgeting analysis. Most financial executives still utilize a goal of maximizing earnings per share and return on equity as their operational goals since they do not believe they can predictably influence the market value of their stock in other ways. The stock market as a whole has a very important influence on all stock prices, and financial executives cannot control this factor.

A number of surveys of financial goals in practice have been conducted over the years, and all of them confirm the fact that managers do not always behave in the shareholders' best interests.[2] Financial theorists counter this tendency by the argument that unless managers do try to maximize shareholder wealth, they will be replaced by the board of directors, who are elected by the shareholders. If the board of directors does not perform this duty, unhappy shareholders—or an outside raider who has purchased shares at depressed prices—will take over voting control and replace both directors and managers. In recent years, a number of well-publicized takeovers lends some credence to this argument, at least in the United States. Even if management is not disciplined by losing their jobs, however, they can be contractually and motivationally influenced to give primacy to the shareholders' interests.

Whether or not U.S. financial executives attempt to maximize shareholder wealth, one needs to recognize that the cultural norms of a multinational firm's foreign employees may not be attuned to this objective. Financial executives who have been educated in other countries are not normally taught that a firm should maximize shareholder wealth. They typically believe the goal should be

---

[1]The focus of attention in the theoretical literature shifted to maximization of market value of a firm's common stock following the pioneering article by Franco Modigliani and Merton Miller, "The Cost of Capital, Corporation Finance, and the Theory of Investment," *American Economic Review,* June 1958, pp. 261–97.

[2]The best recent in-depth study of corporate financial goals can be found in two books that report the results of a 10-year study of 12 large U.S. firms. The books are: Gordon Donaldson and Jay W. Lorsch, *Decision Making at the Top: The Shaping of Strategic Direction* (New York: Basic Books, 1983) and Gordon Donaldson, *Managing Corporate Wealth: The Operation of a Comprehensive Financial Goals System* (New York: Praeger Publishers, 1984).

to maximize the profit of the firm without particular regard to the market value of its stock.

In order to learn what financial executives from outside the Anglo-American environment perceived the financial goal of the firm to be, an international group of academics and practitioners conducted a survey by interviewing financial executives from 87 firms in four manufacturing industries in five countries, including the United States.[3] Exhibit 1.1 is based on the major results of that survey.

Exhibit 1.1 reveals that financial executives in most countries give their highest priority to maximizing the growth rate of earnings per share. This goal was ranked first in France, Japan, the Netherlands, and the United States. Interestingly enough, maximizing the growth rate of earnings per share was not among any of the top five goals in Norway, where guaranteeing the availability of capital was of paramount importance. Guaranteeing the availability of capital was second in importance in France and third in Japan and the Netherlands. For U.S. executives, capital availability seems not to be an important issue—possibly because the developed U.S. money and capital markets make capital availability easy if other goals are attained.

Maximizing return on sales, that is, net income divided by sales, was the only goal ranked within the top five in all five countries. In Japan it was the second goal, in France and Norway it was ranked fourth, and in the Netherlands and the United States it was ranked fifth. Similar to return on sales as a goal is return on investment, measured as net income divided by net worth. Return on investment was mentioned among the top five goals in four of the five countries; only in France was it not among the top five. For the Netherlands, Norway, and the United States, it was the second most important goal; and for Japan, it tied for third place.

In the light of accepted finance theory, it is interesting that financial executives did not rate highly those goals favoring maximizing shareholder wealth. Maximizing share price appreciation plus dividend was third in importance in France and the United States, maximizing market value of shares was ranked fourth in the United States, and maximizing price/earnings ratio was fourth

---

[3]Arthur Stonehill, Theo Beekhuisen, Richard Wright, Lee Remmers, Norman Toy, Antonio Parés, Alan Shapiro, Douglas Egan, and Thomas Bates, "Financial Goals and Debt Ratio Determinants: A Survey of Practice in Five Countries," *Financial Management,* Autumn 1975, pp. 27–41.

EXHIBIT 1.1 Five Most Important Financial Goals for Executives to Maximize, in Five Countries

Rank	France	Japan	Netherlands	Norway	United States
1	Growth of earnings per share* (4.63)†	Growth of earnings per share (2.95)	Growth of earnings per share (3.92)	Availability of capital (3.58)	Growth of earnings per share (4.35)
2	Guaranteed availability of capital (4.25)	Return on sales (2.10)	Return on investment (2.69)	Return on investment (3.73)	Return on investment (2.60)
3	Share price appreciation plus dividend (3.88)	(tie) Return on investment‡ (1.90)	Availability of capital (2.62)	Earnings before interest and taxes (3.42)	Share price appreciation plus dividend (2.40)
4	Return on sales§ (3.63)	(tie) Availability of capital (1.90)	Price/earnings ratio (1.92)	Return on sales (2.77)	Market value of shares (2.50)

5	Earnings before interest and taxes (3.25)	Book value (1.10)	Return on sales (1.69)	Share price appreciation plus dividend (2.12)	Return on sales (2.20)
Sample size	8 firms	20 firms	13 firms	26 firms	20 firms

SOURCE: Adapted from data in A. Stonehill, T. Beekhuisen, R. Wright, L. Remmers, N. Toy, A. Parés, A. Shapiro, D. Egan, and T. Bates, "Financial Goals and Debt Ratio Determinants: A Survey of Practice in Five Countries," *Financial Management*, Autumn 1975, pp. 27–41.

NOTE: Respondents were given a list of 11 variables to be ranked and were invited to write in other financial goals. The list above shows the five most popular goals in each country. Of the 11 suggested goals, 9 are selected at least once in the above listings. Maximizing liquidation value and maximizing cash flow per share did not appear in the top five rankings by executives from any country.

*Variable in cell is the financial characteristic to be maximized.

†Number in cell is the mean rank, where 5 = Most important and 0 = Least important.

‡Return on investment means net income divided by net worth.

§Return on sales means net income divided by sales.

in the Netherlands and fifth in France. Insofar as shareholder wealth maximization is the dominant financial goal advocated in U.S. business schools, its comparative low ranking by practicing American financial executives is especially interesting.

The importance of guaranteed availability of capital in France, the Netherlands, and Norway is indicative of the lack of liquidity and depth in their bond and stock markets. Most of their growth, at least since World War II, has been financed by the commercial banking sector and retained earnings rather than by new issues of stocks and bonds. Thus the importance of maximizing shareholder wealth in these countries is diminished by a lack of dependence on shareholders for new funds.

Japan is an interesting case because it has the second largest stock market in the world, measured both by liquidity and the market value of listed shares. Nevertheless, Japanese firms have mainly financed their growth through bank debt and supplier credit rather than by new stock or bond issues. In fact, Japanese firms have relatively high short-term debt ratios, typically averaging 80 percent in the manufacturing sector compared to 45 percent for all debt for similar U.S. firms.[4]

Another factor governing the Japanese choice of goals is the close cooperation practiced by firms in the same industrial group. For example, a typical group might include companies in steel, shipbuilding, electronics, textiles, and automobiles as well as a bank and a trading company. Furthermore, since the Central Bank would give exceptional support to any important commercial bank that runs into difficulties, these banks can remain very loyal to their client borrowers when they are in trouble. Although each member of the group is independent, they typically own some stock in other group members. The purpose of ownership is not to receive a capital gain or dividends on the stock but rather to show solidarity with the group. In fact, for a group member in Japan to sell its equity position in the other members of the group would be a signal that it wants to leave the group. Therefore, maximizing the market value of a firm's stock may not be an important goal for many Japanese firms. It should be noted, however, that some important Japanese firms (such as Toyota Motors and Sony Corporation) are not members of a group and raise most of their long-term capital abroad. In these cases, they pay more attention to shareholder goals and debt ratio norms in the markets in which they raise their funds.

---

[4]Ibid.

SUMMARY

International finance differs from domestic corporate finance because of the foreign socio-political environment, foreign exchange risk, taxation, and institutional factors.

Finance theory postulates that the goal of the firm should be to maximize the shareholders' wealth. When applied to foreign operations, this goal can be severely constrained by host-country public policy and by the beliefs of the firm's own foreign employees.

The most important host-government constraints are caused by monetary, fiscal, balance of payments, and economic development policies. Political risk can also be a constraint since friendly governments can be superseded by governments unfriendly toward foreign-owned firms.

A survey of financial executives in five countries revealed that they follow a goal of maximizing earnings growth and return on net worth while guaranteeing that funds are always available when needed. Maximizing shareholder wealth was not picked as an important goal by the executives. If this attitude is typical of the foreign employees of a multinational firm, a built-in conflict with the goal proposed by finance theory exists.

ADDITIONAL READINGS

EITEMAN, DAVID K., and ARTHUR STONEHILL. *Multinational Business Finance.* 4th ed. Reading, Mass.: Addison-Wesley Publishing, 1986.

FINDLAY, M. CHAPMAN III, and G. A. WHITMORE. "Beyond Shareholder Wealth Maximization," *Financial Management,* Winter 1974, pp. 25–35.

LESSARD, DONALD R., ed. *International Financial Management, Theory and Applications.* 2nd ed. New York: John Wiley & Sons, 1985.

LEVI, MAURICE. *International Finance: Financial Management and the International Economy.* New York: McGraw-Hill, 1983.

RODRIGUEZ, RITA M., and E. EUGENE CARTER. *International Financial Management.* 3rd ed. Englewood Cliffs, N.J.: Prentice-Hall, 1984.

SHAPIRO, ALAN C. *Multinational Financial Management.* 2nd ed. Boston: Allyn & Bacon, 1986.

STONEHILL, ARTHUR; THEO BEEKHUISEN; RICHARD WRIGHT; LEE REMMERS; NORMAN TOY; ANTONIO PARÉS; ALAN SHAPIRO; DOUGLAS EGAN; and THOMAS BATES. "Financial Goals and Debt Ratio Determinants: A Survey of Practice in Five Countries." *Financial Management,* Autumn 1975, pp. 27–41.

The Foreign Exchange Rates and Markets

This chapter will explain the mechanics of the foreign exchange market and how foreign exchange rates are determined under floating and fixed rate systems. It includes an explanation of foreign exchange quotations, the physical characteristics of the foreign exchange market, and the economic theories that determine exchange rate movements. Management of foreign exchange risk is covered in the next chapter.

FOREIGN EXCHANGE RATES

Foreign exchange is the money of a foreign country. Foreign exchange includes paper money and coins, such as are used by tourists; but, in the world of international finance, foreign exchange usually means bank deposits denominated in various foreign currencies.

Every day major world newspapers, including *The Wall Street Journal,* report foreign exchange quotations. The following quotations for the Swiss franc will be used to explain foreign exchange rates.

Switzerland Franc	U.S. Dollar Equivalent	Foreign Currency per U.S. Dollar
Spot rate	.4520	2.2125
30-day forward	.4541	2.2021
90-day forward	.4585	2.1808
180-day forward	.4654	2.1487

Spot Rates

A *spot transaction* in the interbank market is the purchase of foreign exchange with delivery and payment (referred to as *settlement*) to be completed, normally, on the second following business day. The price at which one currency trades for another in a spot transaction is called the *spot foreign exchange rate* or, more frequently, simply the *spot rate*.

The first line in the above table gives the spot rate. In the United States, the price of one Swiss franc is $.4520, which is to say that the holder of U.S. dollars can purchase one Swiss franc for 45.20 cents. In the United States, this is called a *direct quote*, meaning the price in the home currency (U.S. dollars) equal to one unit of foreign currency. In Switzerland, the price of one U.S. dollar is SF2.2125, meaning that a holder of Swiss francs can buy one U.S. dollar for 2.2125 Swiss francs. In Switzerland, SF2.2125/$ is a direct quote. A quick calculation will reveal that 2.2125 is a reciprocal of .4520:

$$\frac{1}{2.2125} = .4520.$$

The reciprocal of a direct quote is called an *indirect quote*. Thus, the quoted price of SF2.2125/$, which is direct in Switzerland, is indirect when used in the United States.

Because a major portion of the world's foreign exchange trading is between residents of two countries, it is impossible for everyone to express all foreign exchange rates on a direct basis in their own currency. One party to every international transaction must deal in the reciprocal. As a consequence, conventions have developed in which trading between banks, the major portion of the world's foreign exchange trading, is conducted on direct terms in Europe and indirect terms in the United States. A U.S. banker talking to a Swiss banker will state the spot rate as "SF2.2125/$." Indeed, a Japanese banker exchanging dollars for Swiss francs with an Italian banker will also say "SF2.2125/$." The use of the foreign currency price of a U.S. dollar as the worldwide method of quotation is referred to as *European terms*.

One exception to the above is the manner in which quotations for the British pound sterling are expressed. By convention, sterling is always quoted in terms of the number of foreign currency units needed to buy one pound. Thus, in both London and New York (and in Frankfurt and Singapore), the rate between the pound and the dollar will be stated as "$1.4155/£." This custom arose because, for many centuries, sterling was not a decimal currency; prior to 1954, a pound was divided into 20 shillings, and a shilling was divided into 12 pence.

Forward Exchange Rates

A *forward rate* or *forward exchange rate* is the price agreed on *today* for purchase or sale of foreign exchange at a future date. Such a transaction is called a *forward transaction,* and it provides for the transfer *(settlement)* on a designated future date of a specified amount of one currency for a specified amount of another currency. The forward exchange rate is agreed on at the time the contract is made, but payment and delivery are not required until maturity. Forward exchange rates are normally quoted for maturities of 1, 2, 3, 6, and 12 months in the future. The quotations from *The Wall Street Journal,* reproduced above, give forward quotations for the Swiss franc for one month, three months, and six months. Actual settlement dates for forward contracts are based on an even number of months plus two days—that is, a three-month forward contract entered into on January 25th will be settled April 27th or the next following business day if the 27th is a holiday in either country. The description "90 days" is used to mean a three-month contract, even though the actual number of days will be slightly more than 90.

As a matter of terminology, one can speak of "buying forward" or "selling forward" to describe the same event. A forward transaction to deliver dollars for Swiss francs in six months might be called *buying francs forward for dollars* or *selling dollars forward for francs.*

Premiums and Discounts. Forward quotations are either at a premium or a discount from the spot rate. A *premium* means that the direct price in the forward market is higher than the direct price in the spot market, while a *discount* means that the direct forward price is less than the direct spot price. In the quotations above, the three-month forward Swiss franc is quoted (on a direct basis in the United States) at a higher price, $.4585/SF, than the spot price, $.4520. This means that in the United States the forward Swiss franc is more expensive than the spot franc and, therefore, at a premium. Of course, if one were quoting in European terms, the three-month forward quotation is SF2.1808/$, a price that is below the spot rate of SF2.2125/$. One might say that the forward dollar was at a discount.

Outright and Point (Swap) Quotations. An *outright quotation* means the full price is stated. *The Wall Street Journal* reports outright quotations, so the three-month forward quote of SF2.1808/$ is an outright quote. Outright quotations are the form in which most businesspersons and tourists think of foreign exchange rates.

Bankers who trade in foreign exchange on a daily basis express forward exchange rates in terms of *points,* also referred to as the *swap rate.* A point is the difference between the spot rate and the forward rate, carried out to the number of decimal points traditional for trading between the two currencies. Prices between the dollar and most major world currencies are expressed in four decimal points. Major exceptions are the Japanese yen and the Italian lira, which are quoted to only two decimal points on a European terms basis.

The quotations given above can be expressed on a points basis as follows:

	U.S. Dollar Equivalent (American terms)	Foreign Currency per U.S. Dollar (European terms)
Spot rate	.4520	2.2125
30-day forward	+21	−104
90-day forward	+65	−317
180-day forward	+134	−638

Because the point quotation refers to the number of points away from the outright spot rate, the outright spot rate must be known. In the American terms examples above, the 180-day forward quote is 134 points above the spot quote, whereas the 180-day forward European terms quote is 638 points below the spot:

	American Terms	European Terms
Outright spot quote	.4520	2.2125
Plus/minus points	+134	−638
180-day forward	.4654	2.1487

Bids and Asks

The above quotations are in the form of a single quotation; however, actual interbank quotations are stated as a "bid" and an "ask" or "offer." The *bid* represents the price at which the bank will buy foreign exchange from another bank, and the *ask* or *offer* is the price at which the bank will sell. Quotations reported in *The*

Wall Street Journal are interbank (wholesale) ask quotes. Individuals would face less favorable retail quotes.

In the examples using the Swiss franc, then, the actual quotation on a European terms basis might be:

	Bid/Buy	Ask/Offer/Sell
Outright spot rate	2.2110	2.2125
180-day forward	2.1440	2.1487
180-day forward on a points basis	670	638

When a bid-and-ask forward quotation is given on a points basis, the trader need not express the "+" and "−." If the first forward quotation in points (670 above) is greater than the second (638 above), the trader knows to subtract the points from the spot quotation to obtain the outright forward quotation. If the first quotation is smaller than the second, when expressed in points, the points are added to the spot rate to obtain the outright forward rate.

Note that this operating rule applies only to forward quotations *in points;* the outright bid must always be less than the outright ask. (Otherwise, the bank making the quote is giving foreign currency away for less than cost!) This rule works because the additional risk in the forward market causes the spread between bid and ask to be greater than in the spot market.

Forward Quotations in Percentage Terms. Forward quotations are sometimes expressed in terms of an annual percent per annum deviation from the spot rate. This method of quotation facilitates comparing forward premiums or discounts with interest rate differentials. If quotations are given in European terms, and n equals the number of months in the contract, an approximate formula for the percent per annum premium or discount is as follows:

$$\begin{matrix} \text{Forward premium} \\ \text{or discount as a} \\ \text{percent per annum} \\ \text{(European terms)} \end{matrix} = \frac{\text{Spot rate} - \text{Forward rate}}{\text{Forward rate}} \times \frac{12}{n} \times 100.$$

Using the three-month forward ask quotation for the Swiss franc from the quotes given above, we obtain:

$$\begin{matrix} \text{Forward premium} \\ \text{or discount as a} \\ \text{percent per annum} \\ \text{(European terms)} \end{matrix} = \frac{2.2125 - 2.1808}{2.1808} \times \frac{12}{3} \times 100 = +5.8144\%.$$

In the United States, the three-month forward Swiss franc is quoted at a premium of 5.8144 percent per annum.

An alternative equation is used when quotations are given in American terms:

Forward premium or discount as a percent per annum (American terms) $= \dfrac{\text{Forward rate} - \text{Spot rate}}{\text{Spot rate}} \times \dfrac{12}{n} \times 100.$

Applying this formula to the direct quotes for the Swiss franc given earlier, we obtain:

Forward premium or discount as a percent per annum (American terms) $= \dfrac{.4585 - .4520}{.4520} \times \dfrac{12}{3} \times 100 = +5.7522\%.$

The three-month forward Swiss franc is quoted as a premium of 5.7522 percent per annum over the dollar. The slight difference from the previous calculation is caused by rounding; if the American-terms quotations are calculated to seven decimal points as reciprocals of the European-terms quotations, the answers are the same.

Cross Rates

On occasion, a person dealing in foreign exchange will want to obtain an exchange rate between two currencies from their common relationship with a third currency. Suppose, for example, that an American tourist is about to visit Switzerland and cannot find a dollar quotation for the Swiss franc. However, the British pound sterling is quoted in the United States, and the Swiss franc is quoted in London, as follows:

Sterling quote in United States: $1.4155/£
Swiss franc quote in London: SF3.1318/£

The American tourist can exchange $1.4155 for one pound sterling and, with that pound, buy 3.1318 Swiss francs. The exchange rate calculation would be:

$$\frac{\text{Swiss francs per pound}}{\text{Dollars per pound}} = \frac{\text{SF}3.1318/£}{\$1.4155/£} = \text{SF}2.2125/\$$$

Percent Change in Exchange Rates

The amount of depreciation or appreciation caused by a change in exchange rates and expressed as a percentage can be determined from the following formulas. If the exchange rate is expressed in American terms, as in the case of pounds sterling, the formula is as follows. Assume that the pound drops in value from $1.4155/£ to $1.3000/£.

$$\text{Percent change (American terms)} = \frac{\text{Ending rate} - \text{Beginning rate}}{\text{Beginning rate}} \times 100$$

$$= \frac{1.3000 - 1.4155}{1.4155} \times 100 = -8.1597 \text{ percent.}$$

In terms of the U.S. dollar, the pound sterling has dropped in value by 8.1597 percent.

If the exchange rate is given in European terms, as is the case with the Swiss franc, the formula changes. Assume that the Swiss franc rises in value from SF2.2125/$ to SF2.1000/$. Note that if fewer francs are required to purchase a dollar, the Swiss franc is stronger.

$$\text{Percent change (European terms)} = \frac{\text{Beginning rate} - \text{Ending rate}}{\text{Ending rate}} \times 100$$

$$= \frac{2.2125 - 2.1000}{2.1000} \times 100 = +5.3571 \text{ percent.}$$

In terms of the U.S. dollar, the Swiss franc has risen in value by 5.3571 percent.

A drop in foreign exchange rates is often referred to as a "devaluation," especially in the newspapers. The word *devaluation* is sometimes used imprecisely, however. Devaluation properly refers only to a drop in foreign exchange value of a currency that is pegged to gold or to another currency. The opposite of devaluation is *revaluation*. The terms *weakening, deteriorating,* or *depreciating* should be used when the foreign exchange value of a floating currency drops. The opposite of weakening is *appreciating* or *strengthening*, which refer to a gain in the exchange value of a floating currency.

A currency is *soft* when it is expected to drop in value relative to major currencies or if its exchange value is being artificially sustained by its government. A currency is *hard* when it is expected to rise in value relative to major trading currencies.

THE FOREIGN EXCHANGE MARKET

The foreign exchange market is the "meeting place" where bankers, businesspersons, tourists, investors, and others exchange one foreign currency for another. This meeting place is today almost exclusively a system of electronic communications because information about foreign exchange quotes and transactions is transmitted from one location to another via video screens, telephones, telex, and cable. Foreign exchange trading takes place somewhere in the world 24 hours a day, and a very large proportion of trading is conducted between individuals or institutions residing in different countries.

The foreign exchange market consists of (1) the retail market, in which commercial firms and individuals obtain foreign exchange for their business or personal needs, (2) the interbank market, in which the major participants are foreign exchange traders employed by large banks in most countries of the world, (3) brokers, who bring buyers and sellers together for a small commission, (4) speculators, and (5) governments.

Retail customers, such as multinational corporations, importers, and exporters, usually buy and sell foreign exchange through their own bank, which acts as a principal in the transaction by buying or selling customers' foreign exchange for its own account. A retail customer who conducts any significant amount of foreign exchange business will be known to the bank trading department and will simply call that department directly. A purchase or sale in the forward market by a bank customer is, in effect, a credit transaction since the bank is depending on the customer to come up with the money for the transaction at the time of maturity. For this reason, businesses expecting to engage in forward transactions will usually need to have a credit line at their bank. Individuals whose need for foreign exchange is only occasional, such as tourists or one-time investors in foreign securities, usually purchase their foreign exchange at the counter of a bank office.

Participants in the interbank market are primarily foreign exchange traders working for the major banks of the world, although some nonbank foreign exchange traders also deal in this market. In addition, a few of the largest multinational corporations, such as some major oil, entertainment, and automobile companies, have their own trading departments that operate directly in the interbank market. Interbank traders are "dealers" who "make a market" in a technical and operational sense. A dealer must stand willing at all times to quote both a bid and an ask and to deal in from 5 to 10 million dollars, depending on the foreign currency, at the quoted prices. Dealers make their profit by buying foreign exchange at the lower bid price and reselling it at the higher ask price.

A third class of participants in the foreign exchange market is *brokers*. Under some circumstances, a bank will not want to reveal to another interbank participant that it wants to buy or sell a particular currency. To preserve anonymity—and thus not let the knowledge of who is buying or selling influence the quote—the bank seeks the best bid or offer through an independent broker. After the broker matches buyer and seller, the names of the participants are revealed to each other so that settlement can be completed on the prescribed settlement date.

Speculators also participate in the foreign exchange market. Some speculators are themselves traders acting for their bank, while others are individuals. In either case, the speculator is buying or selling foreign exchange in the hope that a price change will result in a profit. The speculator's motives thus differ from those of other participants in that the speculator has no underlying commercial motive for entering the market. Speculators who seek to profit from price differences in different foreign exchange markets are referred to as *arbitragers*.

Central banks, treasuries, and other government agencies sometimes intervene in foreign exchange markets in order to influence particular exchange rates.

FORECASTING EXCHANGE RATES

Supply and demand pressures in the foreign exchange market determine the price of any currency, just as such pressures do in other commodity markets. Supply and demand are a function of such variables as relative inflation and interest rates, but are also influenced by government intervention and the "market sentiment" of speculators, traders, and arbitragers. In order to forecast exchange rates, we will first summarize the international monetary system development since World War II because it provides the rationale for government intervention and market sentiment. Then we will analyze the most important economic variables.

The International Monetary System

Government policy toward foreign exchange rates is influenced by an overall set of international rules agreed on by central bankers. The post–World War II international monetary system was established by an agreement among the Allied Powers reached at Bretton Woods, New Hampshire, in 1944. At that time, it was agreed that after World War II all countries would attempt to maintain fixed exchange rates with respect to gold via their relationship to the U.S. dollar. Only the dollar would continue to be convertible into gold at a price of $35 per ounce of gold. This was called the *gold exchange standard.*

The International Monetary Fund. In order to help countries maintain their exchange rates, the International Monetary Fund (IMF) was established in 1944. It was supposed to lend funds to any member country suffering cyclical, seasonal, or random shocks that would weaken its currency. If the weakness was due to long-term structural problems, however, the country was allowed to devalue its currency while taking other steps to correct the structural problem. The IMF was originally funded by each member subscribing to a quota, but this has since been extended by certain borrowing arrangements with industrial countries and OPEC members. The IMF quotas are currently collectively $92.5 billion, and its borrowing arrangements could raise another $19 billion. Voting power in the IMF is in proportion to each member's quota. Thus, the United States subscribes to about 20 percent of the quota and enjoys 20 percent of the voting rights.

The Crisis of 1971–1973. The gold exchange standard worked fairly well until the 1960s, when the United States began running consistent balance of payments deficits. Although the dollar was used as the main international reserve currency, central banks became saturated with too many dollars and therefore exercised their right to exchange the dollars for gold from the U.S. Treasury. By 1971, the U.S. gold supply had fallen from a high of $26 billion in 1945 to a low of $12 billion. Since foreign central banks held dollars equal to many times the U.S. gold supply, it became obvious that the United States could no longer promise convertibility of dollars into gold. A panic developed in the exchange markets in the summer of 1971. On August 15, 1971, President Nixon suspended convertibility of the dollar to gold, and all currencies were allowed to "float" in relation to the dollar and to each other. "Floating" means that supply and demand for a particular currency determines its price in terms of any other currency.

Some order was restored to the exchange markets in December 1971, when the major industrial countries reached an agreement, later called the "Smithsonian Agreement." The United States agreed to devalue the dollar by 8.57 percent relative to gold and thereby relative to other currencies. Stability was short lived because the United States continued to have balance of payments problems, and confidence in the dollar was low. In February 1973, another run against the dollar forced a second devaluation, this time by 10 percent. Finally, in March 1973, foreign exchange markets closed for several weeks due to chaotic conditions. When they reopened, exchange rates were allowed to float, and the gold exchange standard was at an end. Floating exchange rates were officially condoned by the Jamaica Agreement of 1976, and, at the same time, gold was demonetized. Gold no longer has an official price and is bought and sold by central banks at market prices.

Floating Exchange Rates. From 1973 to the present, exchange rates have been floating with considerable variability. After several attempts to fix exchange rates failed, the members of the Common Market (EEC) agreed in 1979 to establish the European Monetary System. Their currencies now trade in a narrow band relative to each other but float as a bloc relative to the dollar, yen, and other non-EEC currencies. Other countries have tied their own currency to some other currency. For example, a number of countries, particularly in Asia and Latin America, have tied their currency to the U.S. dollar. The present international monetary system, combining fixed and floating exchange rates with periodic unpredictable central bank intervention, complicates the task of forecasting. Nevertheless, in the long run, underlying economic pressures do ultimately determine exchange rates. It so happens that exchange rates, security prices, interest rates, and inflation rates are internationally interdependent and partially mutually determined. Exhibit 2.1 presents a simplified international equilibrium model, which shows how these variables are interrelated, using France and the United States as an example.

Purchasing Power Parity

Purchasing power parity is a well-tested economic theory stating that, in the long run, the differential rate of inflation between two countries will be offset by an equal but opposite change in their exchange rates. Based on the assumptions of Exhibit 2.1 (Relationship A), the French franc should devalue by 5 percent during the coming year because inflation in France is expected to be 5 percent higher than in the United States.

The rationale for purchasing power parity is based on pressure from the balance of payments. If the exchange rate does not change, French goods and services would eventually become more expensive than comparable U.S. goods and services in France, in

---

EXHIBIT 2.1   The International Equilibrium Model

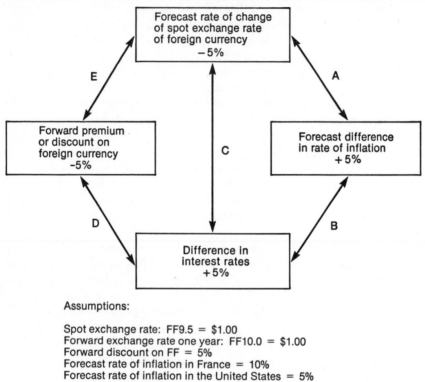

Assumptions:

Spot exchange rate: FF9.5 = $1.00
Forward exchange rate one year: FF10.0 = $1.00
Forward discount on FF = 5%
Forecast rate of inflation in France = 10%
Forecast rate of inflation in the United States = 5%
Interest rate of one-year governments in France = 14%
Interest rate of one-year governments in United States = 9%

---

the United States, and in third countries. For example, assume that a bottle of French Pinot Noir wine starts out at the same price and quality as its California counterpart. Assume further that the price of both wines increases in tandem with domestic inflation. After a year, the French Pinot Noir would be 5 percent more expensive than the California competition, and, after three years, with compounding (5 percent)[3] it would be 16 percent more expensive. At some point, consumers will switch to the California Pinot Noir. It will happen in the United States, in third country markets, and perhaps even in France. This will increase the international demand for U.S. dollars to pay for California wine and decrease the demand for French francs. Other French goods and services will experience the same competitive price disadvantage, and the

French balance of payments on current account will show a deficit. Under freely floating rates, the French franc should depreciate until the original price equilibrium is restored.

Purchasing power parity has been tested empirically numerous times and shown to be reasonably true in the long run for most currencies. However, a few currencies, notably the U.S. dollar, do not seem to respond to balance of payments deficits on current account in the short or medium run because of offsetting movements on the capital account. For example, from 1980 to mid-1985 the dollar was considerably overvalued according to purchasing power parity. This was because the immense inflow of foreign capital to purchase U.S. securities, bank deposits, real estate, and other assets offset record-high U.S. current account deficits and allowed the dollar to remain at its highest levels since the 1960s. Apart from capital account movements, purchasing power parity does not always hold in the short run due to lags in the adjustment process, government interference, and the difficulty of finding comparable price indexes that measure traded goods.

Exhibit 2.2 illustrates both the variability of exchange rates and the fact that purchasing power parity does not hold in the short or medium run. It presents indexes of real bilateral dollar exchange rates between the dollar, deutsche mark, yen, and U.K. pound, all superimposed on a measure of the U.S. balance of payments deficit on current account during the period from 1972–85. Each index measures changes in nominal exchange rates adjusted for related inflation of wholesale prices of finished goods. If purchasing power parity holds, each index should remain at 100 (the December 1971 level). For example, any change in the U.S. dollar/ deutsche mark nominal exchange rate should be just equal to the difference in inflation rates between the United States and Germany. However, Exhibit 2.2 shows that the real exchange rate between the dollar and the deutsche mark (the heaviest line) varied widely from an index value of 100 throughout the period from 1972–85. For example, the dollar was quite undervalued, in a purchasing power sense, in 1973 and again from 1977–80. However, in the period from 1980–85, the dollar strengthened way beyond what could be predicted by purchasing power parity. Similar conclusions can be drawn by observing the indexes for the dollar/yen and dollar/pound real exchange rates.

Fisher Effect

The Fisher effect holds that nominal interest rates in each country are equal to some historical required real rate of return to the

---

EXHIBIT 2.2   Real Bilateral Dollar Exchange Rates and the United States
Current-Account Balance, 1972–1985

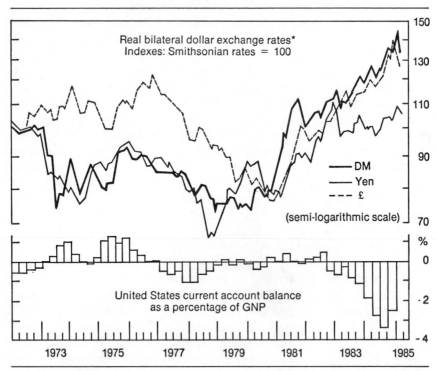

SOURCE: Bank for International Settlements, *Fifty-Fifth Annual Report* (Basle,
Switzerland: June 1985), p. 148.
*Adjusted on the basis of movements in relative wholesale prices of finished
goods.

investor plus a nominal rate of return to compensate for expected
inflation.[1] Exhibit 2.1 (Relationship B) shows that nominal interest
rates in France are 14 percent, leaving investors with a 4 percent
real rate of return after compensation for the 10 percent expected
rate of inflation. The required real rate of return in the United
States is also assumed to be 4 percent with a nominal rate of 9
percent. Therefore, the 5 percent difference in nominal interest
rates in France and the United States is just equal to the difference
in expected inflation rates.

---

[1]The Fisher effect is named after economist Irving Fisher, who first
tested this theory prior to World War II.

The International Fisher Effect

The international Fisher effect (Exhibit 2.1, Relationship C) postulates that the expected change in the spot exchange rate should be in an equal but opposite direction to the difference in interest rates between two countries. Thus, the 5 percent interest differential is matched by an expected 5 percent devaluation of the French franc.

The rationale for the international Fisher effect is based on the need for investors in foreign securities to be compensated for any expected foreign exchange losses. Dollar-based investors who purchase French securities would earn 5 percent more than in comparable U.S. securities but would lose 5 percent when converting the proceeds back to U.S. dollars. However, if investors only expect to lose 4 percent on the foreign exchange conversion, then French securities would be purchased and dollar securities would be sold. If they expect to lose 6 percent on conversion, French securities would be sold and U.S. securities would be purchased.

Interest Rate Parity

The theory of interest rate parity states that a difference in national interest rates for securities of similar risk and maturity should be equal but opposite in sign to the forward exchange rate discount or premium on the foreign currency.[2] Thus, the 5 percent higher French interest rate in Exhibit 2.1 (Relationship D) is equal to the forward discount of 5 percent on French francs.

If interest rate parity did not hold, opportunity exists for an arbitrager to make unlimited risk-free profits from *covered interest arbitrage*. For example, assume the French one-year interest rate on government securities increases to 15 percent, and the forward exchange rate remains unchanged. An opportunity for profit via covered interest arbitrage would exist. Arbitragers all over the world would see the opportunity and would take the following steps. Assume for illustration a $1 million transaction size:

Day 1:
Step 1   Borrow $1 million for one year in the United States at 9 percent per year.

Step 2.   Exchange these dollars to FF9,500,000 at the spot rate of FF9.5 = $1.00.

---

[2]This equality is technically true only after payment of transaction costs, which typically average about one quarter of one percent.

Step 3.   Purchase French government securities of one-year maturity yielding 15 percent per annum.

Step 4.   Sell the expected principal and interest proceeds forward one year at the forward rate of FF10.0 = $1.00. The expected proceeds are the principal of FF9,500,000 plus 15 percent interest of FF1,425,000, or a total of FF10,925,000. (FF10,925,000 ÷ 10 = $1,092,500.)

Step 5.   Pay transaction costs of $250.

One year later:

Step 6.   Receive FF10,925,000 proceeds from investment.

Step 7.   Complete the forward contract by delivering FF10,925,000 at \ FF10.0 per dollar, receiving back $1,092,500.

Step 8.   Repay the $1 million loan plus interest of $90,000.

The net profit on this covered interest arbitrage is calculated as follows:

Proceeds from forward contract (step 7)	$ 1,092,500
Less cost of dollar loan (step 8)	(1,090,000)
Less transaction costs (step 5)	(250)
Net profit before taxes	$ 2,250

The net profit earned in this example of covered interest arbitrage is $2,250. This is a riskless profit as long as the bank honors its forward contract and the French government does not default on its bonds. Such a riskless profit will attract a huge influx of dollars to purchase French securities and a reversing sale forward of French francs. As a result, the French franc forward rate discount should widen in response to the forward sale of francs, and the interest rate on French government securities should decline in response to the extra demand for them. These actions should continue until there is no more incentive to purchase French securities. At that point, interest rate parity would have been restored.

The Forward Rate as an Unbiased Predictor of the Future Spot Rate

Financial managers of business firms often want to forecast future exchange rates. Sometimes this is to anticipate the cost in one currency of selling goods at a price in another currency or to anticipate the home currency cost of repaying a foreign currency loan. At other times, the motivation is to estimate the home currency cash flows to be received from a long-term capital investment project in a foreign currency. The interaction of purchasing power parity, the Fisher effect, the international Fisher effect, and interest rate parity provide such a forecast.

If foreign exchange markets are efficient, some empirical studies show that the forward rate is the best unbiased predictor of the future spot rate. This is shown in Exhibit 2.1, Relationship E. The rationale is that all investors would have access to all the relevant information, and bankers would be willing to buy or sell forward contracts. There is no reason to believe a priori that either sellers or buyers are going to consistently forecast the actual future spot exchange rate. They are as likely to forecast too high as too low. Therefore, the forward rate is likely to be a consensus forecast. In effect, it is the unbiased mean value (with a very large standard deviation) of a whole range of predicted future spot rates.

The forward rate is not necessarily an accurate predictor, and some recent empirical studies have found better predictors. However, studies of foreign exchange forecasting services have concluded that, on the average, their predictions do not significantly outperform the forward rate, although some individual firms have predicted consistently better than the average.

Government Intervention

The international equilibrium model illustrated in Exhibit 2.1 works best when foreign exchange rates are freely floating without government interference. However, some governments, such as those in the European Monetary System Agreement, are required to intervene to influence exchange rates that are supposed to be stabilized. Government intervention prevents movement toward equilibrium if central banks are willing to accept losses in order to counter market pressures. At some point, however, the price of stabilization becomes too high, and exchange rates are allowed to change. The key to forecasting managed or fixed exchange rates is to understand this political process and to judge the determination of central bankers to maintain a disequilibrium exchange rate. This is difficult because government officials quite naturally do not announce their intentions to devalue or revalue a currency.

SUMMARY

In this chapter, we have explained the mechanics of the foreign exchange market, including quotations of spot and forward rates, premiums and discounts on forward rates, and market participants. The international monetary system was described as background for the task of forecasting exchange rates. The international equilibrium model was analyzed because it shows how exchange rates, interest rates, and inflation rates are interrelated and mutually determined. We summarized the theories underlying this model, including purchasing power parity, the Fisher effect, the international Fisher effect, interest rate parity, covered interest arbitrage, and the forward rate as an unbiased predictor of the future spot rate. In countries that attempt to fix exchange rates relative to a reference exchange rate, government intervention is required. Predicting the politics of devaluation is difficult but necessary because it overrides the economic determinants in the short run.

ADDITIONAL READINGS

AGMON, TAMIR, ROBERT G. HAWKINS, and RICHARD M. LEVICH, eds. *The Future of the International Monetary System.* Lexington, Mass.: Lexington Books, 1984.

CORNELL, BRADFORD, and MARC R. REINGANUM. "Forward and Future Prices." *Journal of Finance,* December 1981, pp. 1035–45.

CUMBY, ROBERT E., and MAURICE OBSTFELD. "A Note on Exchange Rate Expectations and Nominal Interest Differentials: A Test of the Fisher Hypothesis." *Journal of Finance,* June 1981, pp. 697–703.

FRENKEL, JACOB A., and RICHARD M. LEVICH. "Covered Interest Arbitrage: Unexploited Profits?" *Journal of Political Economy,* April 1975, pp. 325–38.

GIDDY, IAN. "Measuring the World Foreign Exchange Market." *Columbia Journal of World Business,* Winter 1979, pp. 36–48.

———. "Foreign Exchange Options." *Journal of Futures Markets,* Summer 1983, pp. 143–66.

GOLDSTEIN, HENRY. "Foreign Currency Futures: Some Further Aspects." Federal Reserve Bank of Chicago, *Economic Perspectives,* November–December 1983, pp. 3–13.

HUTCHINSON, MICHAEL, and CHARLES PIGOTT. "Budget Deficits, Exchange Rates, and the Current Account: Theory and U.S. Experience." Federal Reserve Bank of San Francisco, *Economic Review,* Fall 1984, pp. 5–25.

JACQUE, LAURENT L. "Why Hedgers Are Not Speculators." *Columbia Journal of World Business,* Winter 1979, pp. 108–16.

KOVEOS, PETER, and BRUCE SEIFERT. "Purchasing Power Parity and Black Markets." *Financial Management,* Autumn 1985, pp. 40–46.

KUBARYCH, ROGER M. *Foreign Exchange Markets in the United States.* Rev. ed. New York: Federal Reserve Bank of New York, 1983.

LOGUE, DENNIS E., and GEORGE S. OLDFIELD. "What's so Special about Foreign Exchange Markets?" *Journal of Portfolio Management,* Spring 1977, pp. 19–24.

RIEHL, HEINZ, and RITA RODRIGUEZ. *Foreign Exchange and Money Markets.* New York: McGraw-Hill, 1983.

RUCK, ADAM. "Understanding Foreign Exchange Trading." *Euromoney,* April 1981, pp. 117–24.

WALMSLEY, JULIAN. "The New York Foreign Exchange Market." *Bankers Magazine* (US), January–February 1984, pp. 67–69.

WILLIAMSON, JOHN. *The Exchange Rate System.* Washington, DC: Institute for International Economics, September 1983.

PROBLEMS

The problems below are based on the following foreign exchange quotations as they might appear in the financial pages of a newspaper.

	Britain $/£	Canada · C$/US$	Japan ¥/$	France FF/$	Germany DM/$
Spot	1.4145	1.4199	192.65	7.2815	2.3755
30-day forward	1.4097	1.4229	192.35	7.2860	2.3690
90-day forward	1.3987	1.4290	191.74	7.2970	2.3550
180-day forward	1.3843	1.4359	180.87	7.3070	2.3360

1. What is the direct spot quote in the United States of each of the spot rates given above?

2. Is the three-month forward Canadian dollar at a premium or discount relative to the U.S. dollar? By what annual percentage?

3. Express the one-, three-, and six-month forward French franc quotes on a points basis. Indicate "premium" or "discount" for the quotation.

4. What is the spot exchange rate between Japanese yen and West German marks?

5. You read in the financial press that the British pound has fallen 22 percent over the last decade. What was the spot quote a decade ago?

6. The U.S. three-month Treasury bill rate is 8 percent per annum. Estimate the U.K. three-month Treasury bill rate.

7. Exchange rates are: DM2.3755/$ spot
   DM2.2925/$ one-year forward

   Interest rates are: 8 percent per annum in Germany
   10 percent per annum in the United States

   You have no money, but your credit is good for a loan of $10,000 or its equivalent in German marks. You can borrow or invest dollars for one year at 10 percent, and you can borrow or invest marks for one year at 8 percent.

   You notice that U.S. interest rates are above German rates, and you would like to earn excess profits with no risk. What can you do, and how much can you earn?

CHAPTER THREE

Foreign Exchange Risk Management

A multinational firm with foreign currency assets or liabilities or one carrying out transactions that involve making or receiving future payments in foreign currencies will be influenced by changes in the value of those currencies relative to the home currency. Foreign exchange risk arises because of the possibility that a firm will lose or gain when foreign exchange rates change. Foreign exchange risk *management* deals with techniques to reduce or eliminate foreign exchange risk.

A cost is usually incurred to reduce foreign exchange risk, so a manager must select techniques that will not only reduce risk but also maximize the value of the firm to its owners in the long run. In some instances, the cost of risk reduction may be greater than the added value to the firm from having the risk removed. Some risk reduction techniques are explained in this chapter, while others come about as part of the normal operation of a multinational firm and are considered throughout other chapters of this book.

"Exposure" is a measure of foreign exchange risk. Multinational financial managers are forever confronted by the dilemma that three different types of exposure exist, each of which measures a different kind of foreign exchange risk. Techniques that minimize one type of risk may increase another.

1. *Translation exposure,* sometimes called *accounting exposure,* measures the impact of an exchange rate change on the financial statements of a firm. An example would be the impact of an Italian lira devaluation on a U.S. firm's reported net income and balance sheet.

2. *Transaction exposure* measures potential gains or losses on the future settlement of outstanding obligations that are denominated in a foreign currency. An example would be a U.S. dollar loss after the lira devalues, on payment received for an export invoiced in lira before that devaluation.
3. *Economic exposure* is the potential for change in the present value of future cash flows due to an *unexpected* change in an exchange rate. An example would be the cash flow change caused by the unexpected increase in value of the U.S. dollar between 1980 and 1985. The rise in the dollar caused lowered earnings for U.S. firms that depended on export markets or competed domestically with foreign imports.

In the remainder of this chapter, each of these types of exposure will be defined in greater detail, ways of measuring them will be suggested, and possible management responses will be discussed.

TRANSLATION (ACCOUNTING) EXPOSURE

Translation exposure arises because parent firms must consolidate financial statements of their foreign affiliates into their parent statement. Because affiliate financial statements are usually prepared in foreign currency terms, that statement must be "translated," that is, restated in home currency terms, before its components can be added to the account balances of the parent firm. If exchange rates change, the "value" as measured in the home currency will also change and will produce either a gain or a loss relative to the translation of the prior period. Depending on the accounting rules in effect at the time, this translation gain or loss will be either added to or subtracted from net income in the income statement or carried directly to the shareholders' equity section of the balance sheet.

In the United States, rules that govern how foreign currency statements must be translated are set out in *Statement of Financial Accounting Standards Number 52*, sometimes called *FAS 52* or *SFAS 52*, issued in December 1981 by the Financial Accounting Standards Board (FASB), the organization that establishes accounting standards for audited financial statements.

Current (1986) FASB rules require translation by the *current rate* method. Prior to 1981, U.S. companies were governed by *FAS 8*, which required use of the *temporal* method, also referred to in a more general sense as the *monetary/nonmonetary* method. A *current/noncurrent* method is also used in some countries. We will focus on the current rate method because it is now accepted practice in the United States.

Under the current rate method, all balance sheet assets and liabilities are translated at the current rate of exchange in effect on the balance sheet date. Income statement accounts are usually translated at an average exchange rate for the reporting period. Dividends are translated at the exchange rate when paid. All equity accounts are translated at the historical exchange rates that were in effect at the time the accounts first entered the balance sheet.

Calculating Translation Exposure

Translation exposure can best be illustrated with an example. Assume that a foreign affiliate has been in operation for several years. The exchange rate of four pesos (Ps) per dollar has not changed in recent years. The foreign affiliate's books are kept in pesos.

The affiliate's balance sheet in pesos as translated into dollars is as follows:

Balance Sheet
December 31, 1986
(in thousands)

	Pesos	Translation Rate (Ps/$1)	Dollars
Cash	Ps 3,600	4/1	$ 900
Accounts receivable	4,800	4/1	1,200
Inventory	4,800	4/1	1,200
Net plant and equipment	6,000	4/1	1,500
	Ps19,200		$4,800
Bank loan	Ps 2,400	4/1	$ 600
Long-term loan	3,600	4/1	900
Common stock equity	13,200	4/1	3,300
	Ps19,200		$4,800

The translation procedure consists of dividing each peso account by the exchange rate in pesos per dollar to obtain a measure of the "dollar value" of each account. The translated values of assets and liabilities (in the right column above) are added to the parent's own dollar accounts to create a consolidated balance sheet.

Assume that on the morning after the above translation, the peso devalues to Ps5/$, and that the firm immediately prepares a new balance sheet. Under the current rate method, all assets and all liabilities are translated at the new current rate. Common stock equity is still translated at its historic rate. Any imbalance in the translated statement is recorded in the equity section of the balance sheet under a separate heading, Cumulative Translation Adjustment Account. The new balance sheet translated the following day would appear as follows:

**Balance Sheet
January 1, 1987
(in thousands)**

	Pesos	Translation Rate (Ps/$1)	Dollars
Cash	Ps 3,600	5/1	$ 720
Accounts receivable	4,800	5/1	960
Inventory	4,800	5/1	960
Net plant and equipment	6,000	5/1	1,200
	Ps19,200		$3,840
Bank loan	Ps 2,400	5/1	$ 480
Long-term loan	3,600	5/1	720
Common stock equity	13,200	4/1	3,300
Cumulative translation adjustment			(660)
	Ps19,200		$3,840

The firm experiences a translation loss of $660,000. Under the rules of *FAS 52*, this loss does not flow through the income statement or cause a drop in reported net income. Rather, the loss is recorded in the Cumulative Translation Adjustment account in the equity section of the balance sheet. Consequently, it reduces shareholders' equity, which now becomes $3,300,000 − $660,000 = $2,640,000.

The loss of $660,000 can be analyzed as follows:

Decrease in the dollar value of cash balances from $900,000 to $720,000:	$ 180,000 loss
Decrease in the dollar value of accounts receivable from $1,200,000 to $960,000:	240,000 loss
Decrease in the dollar value of inventory from $1,200,000 to $960,000:	240,000 loss
Decrease in the dollar value of net plant and equipment from $1,500,000 to $1,200,000:	300,000 loss

Gain from drop in the dollar value of bank loan from $600,000 to $480,000:	− 120,000 gain
Gain from drop in the dollar value of long-term loan from $900,000 to $720,000:	− 180,000 gain
Net loss	$ 660,000

The net loss may also be calculated as a drop in the value of "net exposed assets" equal to the percent devaluation of the local currency. Using the formula described in Chapter Two, the percentage change equals

$$\frac{\text{Beginning rate} - \text{Ending rate}}{\text{Ending rate}} \times 100 =$$

$$\frac{4 - 5}{5} \times 100 = -20 \text{ percent, that is,}$$
$$\text{a 20 percent devaluation.}$$

Under the current rate method, all assets and all liabilities are exposed. Net exposed assets is the difference:

	In Pesos	In Dollars
Value of exposed assets	Ps 19,200,000	$ 4,800,000
Value of exposed liabilities	− 6,000,000	− 1,500,000
Net exposed assets	Ps 13,200,000	$ 3,300,000
times percentage devaluation	× .20	× .20
Translation loss	Ps 2,640,000	$ 660,000

Under most conditions, the translation loss would be viewed as the dollar amount because the purpose of the calculation is to measure the impact on the parent firm's consolidated financial statement. Nevertheless, exposure can also be viewed from a local currency perspective, which is helpful when thinking of financial policies to reduce exposure. Note that Ps2,640,000 divided by the beginning exchange rate of Ps4/$ is $660,000.

Under other translation methods, accounts considered exposed are different, with the result that the measured amount of translation loss will also be different, even when the actual economic circumstances are identical.

Reducing Translation Exposure with a Balance Sheet Hedge

A balance sheet hedge involves either reducing exposed assets to equal exposed liabilities or increasing exposed liabilities to equal exposed assets. If exposed assets equal exposed liabilities, any exchange rate change would change the value of exposed assets and liabilities in equal but opposite directions, leaving the value of the equity portion of the statement unchanged. Consider again the peso balance sheet of December 31, 1986, referred to earlier.

Balance Sheet
December 31, 1986
(in thousands of pesos)

Cash	Ps 3,600	⎫		
Accounts receivable . .	4,800	⎬		
Inventory	4,800	⎬	Exposed assets	Ps 19,200
Net plant and		⎬		
equipment	6,000	⎭		
	Ps19,200			
Bank loan	Ps 2,400	⎱	Less exposed	
Long-term loan	3,600	⎰	liabilities	−6,000
Common stock				
equity	13,200			
	Ps19,200		Net exposure	Ps 13,200

Exposed assets can be reduced by several techniques. Peso cash balances can be exchanged for dollar balances if this is allowed by local foreign exchange authorities. Accounts receivable generated by sales denominated in pesos can be gradually replaced with dollar receivables if sales can instead be denominated in dollars. If most of the firm's customers are local, this is probably not possible. However, if the firm exports to world markets, dollar-denominated sales, and thus receivables, might be possible. Inventory levels could be reduced, and the investment in plant and equipment might be reduced by selling those fixed assets and then leasing them back. All of these actions would reduce exposed assets, but concern must be given as to whether they would impair operational competitiveness or efficiency as well.

Exposed liabilities can be increased by borrowing pesos from local banks or by raising long-term debt denominated in pesos. However, the peso proceeds of any additional borrowing must immediately be exchanged for dollars. If this is not done, the firm has merely increased exposed liabilities and exposed assets (cash) by the same amount, with no impact on net exposure. If the local firm is not allowed to hold dollar cash balances, the newly borrowed pesos might be exchanged for dollars to remit dividends, license fees, or repayments on dollar-denominated debts. The wisdom of additional peso borrowing also depends on the cost of the loans relative to the cost of borrowing other currencies.

Reducing Exposure with a Forward Market Hedge

A second general approach to reducing translation exposure is to hedge the potential translation loss in the forward exchange market. This approach is risky. To attempt this hedge, the firm should sell local currency forward, the amount being determined by the following formula (where LC means any local currency):

$$\begin{matrix} \text{Forward contract} \\ \text{size in local} \\ \text{currency units} \end{matrix} = \frac{\text{Expected translation loss (in \$)}}{\underset{\text{(in \$/LC)}}{(\text{Forward rate})} - \underset{\text{(in \$/LC)}}{(\text{Expected future spot rate})}}.$$

For the firm referred to earlier, the exchange rate changed from Ps4/\$ to Ps5/\$, that is, from \$.25/Ps to \$.20/Ps. Assume that the forward exchange rate was \$.23/Ps, that is, Ps4.3478+/\$. The size of the forward contract would be:

$$\text{Forward contract size} = \frac{\$660,000}{.23 - .20} = \text{Ps22,000,000.}$$

If the affiliate sold Ps22,000,000 forward and if its expectations were correct about the future spot rate, the results would be as follows:

- Today: Sell pesos forward at \$.23/Ps:
  Ps22,000,000 × .23 = \$5,060,000 to receive at maturity.
- Maturity: Buy pesos spot at \$.20/Ps:
  Ps22,000,000 × .20 = \$4,400,000 to pay out at maturity.
- Profit: \$5,060,000 − \$4,400,000 = \$660,000.

This profit of \$660,000 would exactly offset the translation loss. In the United States, as in most countries, profit on purchase and sale of an asset is taxable. However, translation losses are not realized and so are not tax deductible. If the income tax rate was 46 percent, offsetting a translation loss of \$660,000 would require a pretax profit of \$660,000/.54 = \$1,222,222. The forward contract would therefore have to be Ps22,000,000/.54 = Ps40,740,740! Use of the forward market to offset an anticipated translation loss is risky because the approach amounts to speculating in the forward market in the hope that profit on the speculation will be the same as the translation loss. (The suggestion is sometimes made that if the firm is so clever that it can speculate successfully on a consistent basis, it should concentrate on speculation and quit its normal business!) For example, if at the end of the attempted hedge above, the spot market had been $.24/Ps instead of $.20/Ps, the results would have been:

- Today: Sell pesos forward at $.23/Ps:
              Ps22,000,000 × .23 = $5,060,000 to receive at
              maturity.
- Maturity: Buy pesos spot at $.24/Ps:
              Ps22,000,000 × .24 = $5,280,000 to pay out at
              maturity.
- Loss: $5,060,000 − $5,280,000 = $220,000!

In addition, the firm would have experienced a different translation loss caused by the drop in the exchange rate from Ps5/$ to the new ending rate of Ps4.1667/$ (1/.24 = 4.1667). The amount of devaluation would now be 4 percent, and the translation loss would be $3,300,000 × .04 = $132,000 (i.e., Net exposed assets × Percentage devaluation = Translation loss). The total loss would be $132,000 + $220,000 = $352,000.

Consequences of Doing Nothing

The translation loss in the example above is a nonrealized or "paper" loss. Although it influences the size of the parent firm's equity accounts, it does *not* represent a cash loss. Under provisions of *FAS 52* in the United States, the translation loss does not pass through reported earnings; however, this attribute does not necessarily apply in other countries.

Most attempts to hedge translation loss have a cost. Forward market hedges are speculative and have a cost in terms of spreads paid to the banks. Balance sheet hedges might cause operating inefficiencies, distorted local debt/equity ratios, and increased interest cost. Therefore, most firms today do not try to offset translation exposure but do keep it in mind when deciding on the amount of local financing to employ.

A reasonable policy, then, would seem to be to ignore forward hedges, plan an affiliate's capital structure so that equity is as minimal as permitted by other criteria, and accept the translation consequences that follow without focusing on translation exposure to the exclusion of transaction exposure and economic exposure—both of which involve actual cash flows.

TRANSACTION EXPOSURE

Transaction exposure is a firm's vulnerability to loss, or its chance of gain, when an outstanding obligation incurred in a foreign currency is paid off. The most common unsettled obligations are foreign exchange to be paid for imports or to be received for exports. Other unsettled obligations arise from the purchase of services on credit and because of borrowing or lending denominated in foreign currencies. A firm may also have a transaction gain or loss because of obligations incurred under outstanding forward foreign exchange contracts.

Transaction Exposure Example

Assume Boeing sells a new aircraft to Air France. The sales price for the aircraft is $40 million; and, since the current exchange rate is FF7/$, Boeing sells the aircraft for FF280 million. Payment is to be made in francs six months after the date of sale.

If, on payment date, the exchange rate is FF8/$, Air France will remit FF280 million, which Boeing will exchange for $35 million. Because Boeing had booked an account receivable of $40 million and only received $35 million, it experiences a *transaction loss* of $5 million. This loss is a realized loss for both accounting and tax purposes, meaning that Boeing is out of pocket $5 million, which it had already booked as profit at the time of sale and expected to receive. The $5 million loss will reduce Boeing's profit for the year but will also reduce its income taxes. Transaction losses differ in this respect from translation losses, which do not influence taxable income.

Proceeds from the sale might well have ended up being some other amount. Had the ending spot exchange rate been FF6.8/$, for example, Boeing would have received $41,176,470, which is more than the $40 million booked as an account receivable. If the exchange rate fell to FF9/$, Boeing would have received only $31,111,111. In other words, the ending proceeds are at risk and could be the same as, greater than, or less than the expected dollar amount.

Boeing could have avoided the exchange risk by insisting that payment for the aircraft be in dollars. This does not eliminate the risk but simply transfers the risk from the seller to the buyer. If Air France was obligated to pay $40 million, the cost in francs would be FF320 million if the spot exchange rate in six months was FF8/$ but only FF272 million if the exchange rate was FF6.8/$. Which currency is used as the currency of denomination for a credit sale is a matter of negotiation between the two parties.

However, whoever assumes the foreign exchange risk will include the cost of offset in calculating the true price of the aircraft.

Hedging Transaction Exposure in the Forward Market

Assume that on the day the aircraft is sold for FF280 million, the six-month forward rate for the French franc is FF7.2/$. Boeing could sell FF280 million forward six months at FF7.2/$ and, in six months, receive $38,888,888. The advantage of such a forward contract is that the dollar proceeds of the sale are certain: the proceeds will be $38,888,888—neither more nor less. Boeing has no further foreign exchange risk. The disadvantage is that Boeing receives fewer dollars—in this instance, $38,888,888 instead of $40 million. The difference, $1,111,112, can be regarded as the amount forgone in order to have a certain sum ($38,888,888) instead of an uncertain sum ($40 million).

Of course, Boeing should have considered the $1,111,112 cost of the hedge in setting the price of the aircraft. Boeing could have raised its price to FF288 million. If this amount was sold forward at FF7.2/$, it could have yielded exactly $40 million, the amount Boeing wanted in dollars. However, at the higher price of FF288 million, Air France might not have purchased the aircraft! Clearly, the cost of foreign exchange protection is a component of the total bargaining process.

Hedging Transaction Exposure in the Money Market

An alternative would be for Boeing to borrow enough French francs against the account receivable so that repayment of the principal and interest in six months would be FF280 million. Assuming an interest rate of 10 percent per annum, or 5 percent for six months, the amount to be borrowed would be:

$$\frac{FF280,000,000}{1.05} = FF266,666,666.$$

Boeing would borrow FF266,666,666 on the day of sale and would immediately exchange it at the spot rate (FF7/$), receiving $38,095,237. Six months from the date of sale, Boeing would receive FF280 million from Air France and would use that sum to repay both the principal and interest on the loan.

The sum of $38,095,237 received today is assured and thus risk free, but it is less than the $38,888,888 that could be received via the forward market hedge. However, it is received at the present time rather than six months hence. Whether or not Boeing would prefer $38,095,237 today or $38,888,888 in six months depends on its opportunity cost of funds. If Boeing could use funds for six months at anything in excess of 4.1667 percent per annum, or 2.0833 percent for six months, it would prefer the smaller present sum. The break-even investment rate for six months is calculated as follows:

$$\$38,095,237X = \$38,888,888$$

$$X = 1.020833 \text{ or } 2,0833 \text{ percent.}$$

One should not conclude from the above example that a money market hedge is always more advantageous than a forward market hedge. Indeed, if interest rate parity holds, both hedges should have about the same market cost. The choice of which hedge to take will depend on the opportunity cost of funds to the firm as well as whether local borrowing is actually available.

Other Hedging Techniques.   Transaction exposure may also be hedged by the use of foreign currency options. As this is an advanced technique, it will not be explained here but is explained in international financial management textbooks.

An Unhedged Posture

Another alternative would be for Boeing to remain unhedged. As was shown in the beginning of the example, this could result in more, less, or the same ending dollar proceeds, depending on the spot rate in six months. If one believes that exchange markets are efficient and that forward rates are the best indicator of future spot rates, one should expect that the unhedged alternative would lead to the same results as the forward market hedge. In a probabilistic sense, this may be correct, although conflicting evidence exists that forward exchange rates are in fact unbiased predictors of future spot rates. However, even if the expected ending proceeds are the same, the risk is different. The forward and money market hedges give a *certain* ending result, while under the best of conditions the unhedged alternative allows a great deal of *variation* about a most likely result that is the same. For this reason, many firms will hedge in the forward market or the money market in order to reduce their transaction risk—that is, the variability of expected results.

ECONOMIC EXPOSURE

Economic exposure is the possibility that an unexpected change in exchange rates will cause a change in the future cash flows of a firm and that, as a consequence, the value of the firm (measured as the present value of expected future cash flows) will change. Economic exposure differs from translation and transaction exposures in that it is a subjective concept that is not easily measured. On the other hand, economic exposure is vastly more important in the long run than either translation or transaction exposure.

An Economic Exposure Example

Economic exposure can be understood only in a probabilistic sense. Suppose that with no change in the exchange rate, General Motors expects its Belgian parts manufacturing affiliate to earn net profits of BF500 million per year forever. The annual provision for depreciation is assumed to equal the annual cost of replacing plant assets, so cash flow is equal to net income. The exchange rate is currently BF50/$, so Belgian franc earnings are expected to be equivalent to $10 million per year. Investors discount General Motors' foreign earnings at 16 percent per annum. Therefore, the value of the Belgian affiliate is:

$$\frac{\$10,000,000}{.16} = \$62,500,000.$$

If the exchange rate unexpectedly drops in value to BF55/$, earnings of BF500 million or $9,090,909 will be worth only $56,818,182 instead of $62,500,000. Investors might conclude that the value of the affiliate had dropped because its Belgian franc earnings were suddenly worth fewer dollars.

Imagine, however, that with the lower value of the Belgian franc the Belgian affiliate of General Motors is able, within a short time, to compete more effectively, both for exports and against foreign imports entering Belgium. Local direct costs (labor and material) do not immediately increase when the local currency devalues, so the affiliate's costs relative to competitors in other countries drop. These forces lead to a sales volume increase. Overhead (which also did not increase in Belgian franc terms when the Belgian franc devalued) is now spread over a greater volume, increasing the net profit margin. As a consequence, local currency profit quickly rises to BF605 million, or BF605,000,000/55 = $11,000,000 profit per year. If shareholders do not perceive that the firm's risk has changed, the value of the foreign affiliate will now be:

$$\frac{\$11,000,000}{.16} = \$68,750,000.$$

The devaluation led to an *increase* in the foreign affiliate's value. The point is that the "true" value of the affiliate is the discounted present value of future net cash flows. A devaluation will affect these flows, but prior to or at the time of devaluation that effect can be estimated only with difficulty.

Managing Economic Exposure

Since *unexpected* changes in exchange rates cannot be predicted, the best strategy to manage economic exposure is to diversify operations and financing internationally. Operational diversification implies that the sales, location of production, and raw material sources should be diversified into different countries. Diversifying sources of financing implies that a firm should have access to both domestic and international capital markets.

If a firm diversifies internationally, management is prepositioned to react to the unexpected changes in exchange rates that cause disequilibrium conditions to exist in the foreign exchange, money, and product markets. In other words, there are times when purchasing power parity or the international Fisher effect do not behave according to theory. At those times, profits can be increased by shifting sales, sources of production, or financing, depending on relative prices and costs. Production can be increased in countries whose currency is undervalued. Sales efforts can be increased in countries with overvalued currencies. Long-term capital can be raised in countries where the real interest rate is temporarily low. The key is not to predict disequilibrium conditions but rather to recognize them when they occur and be prepositioned to react to disequilibrium opportunities as they arise.

SUMMARY

In this chapter, we have looked at three types of foreign exchange exposure: translation, transaction, and economic. Although economic exposure is the most important, it is also subjective, whereas translation and transaction exposures can be measured precisely.

In addition to discussing how to measure these three types of exposure, we have discussed operational ways to minimize the risk associated with each. Translation exposure may be minimized with balance sheet hedges, and a possible but risky attempt may be made to reduce translation exposure through the forward exchange market. Transaction exposure may be reduced by either a forward hedge or a money market hedge. Economic exposure should be viewed as an opportunity to take advantage of unexpected exchange rate changes. To take advantage of disequilibrium situations, the firm should already have diversified itself internationally, both in terms of its operations and its access to financial markets.

ADDITIONAL READINGS

ADLER, MICHAEL. "Exposure to Currency Risk: Definition and Measurement." *Financial Management,* Spring 1984, pp. 41–50.

BABBEL, DAVID F. "Determining the Optimum Strategy for Hedging Currency Exposure." *Journal of International Business Studies,* Spring/Summer 1983, pp. 133–39.

BATRA, RAVEENDRA N.; SHABTAI DONNENFELD; and JOSEF HADAR. "Hedging Behavior by Multinational Firms." *Journal of International Business Studies,* Winter 1982, pp. 59–70.

BEIDLEMAN, CARL R. *Financial Swaps: New Strategies in Currency and Coupon Risk Management.* Homewood, Ill.: Dow Jones-Irwin, 1985.

DONALDSON, HOWARD, and ALAN REINSTEIN. "Implementing *FAS No. 52:* The Critical Issues." *Financial Executive,* June 1983, pp. 40–50.

DUFEY, GUNTER. "Corporate Finance and Exchange Rate Variations." *Financial Management,* Summer 1972, pp. 51–57.

DUFEY, GUNTER, and S. L. SRINIVASULU. "The Case for Corporate Management of Foreign Exchange Risk." *Financial Management,* Winter 1983, pp. 54–62.

EAKER, MARK R. "Denomination Decision for Multinational Transactions." *Financial Management,* Autumn 1980, pp. 23–29.

————."The Numeraire Problem and Foreign Exchange Risk." *Journal of Finance,* May 1981, pp. 419–26.

Statement of Financial Accounting Standards No. 52, "Foreign Currency Translation." Stamford, Conn.: Financial Accounting Standards Board, 1981.

FLOOD, EUGENE, JR., and DONALD R. LESSARD. "On the Management of Operating Exposure to Exchange Rates: A Conceptual Approach." *Financial Management,* Spring 1986, pp. 25–36.

GIDDY, IAN H. "Why It Doesn't Pay to Make a Habit of Forward Hedging." *Euromoney,* December 1976, pp. 96–100.

————. "Exchange Risk: Whose View?" *Financial Management,* Summer 1977, pp. 23–33.

HAGEMANN, HELMUT. "Anticipate Your Long-Term Foreign Exchange Risks." *Harvard Business Review,* March/April 1977, pp. 81–88.

HEKMAN, CHRISTINE R. "A Financial Model of Foreign Exchange Exposure." *Journal of International Business Studies,* Summer 1985, pp. 83–99.

————. "Foreign Exchange Exposure: Accounting Measures and Economic Exposure." *Journal of Cash Management,* February/March 1983, pp. 34–45.

JACQUE, LAURENT L. "Management of Foreign Exchange Risk: A Review Article." *Journal of International Business Studies,* Spring/Summer 1981, pp. 81–101.

LEVI, MAURICE D. "Underutilization of Forward Markets or Rational Behavior." *Journal of Finance,* September 1979, pp. 1013–17.

LOGUE, DENNIS E., and GEORGE S. OLDFIELD. "Managing Foreign Assets When Foreign Exchange Markets Are Efficient." *Financial Management,* Summer 1977, pp. 16–22.

PARK, YOON S. "Currency Swaps as a Long-Term International Financing Technique." *Journal of International Business Studies,* Winter 1984, pp. 47–54.

RODRIGUEZ, RITA M. "Corporate Exchange Risk Management: Theme and Abberations." *Journal of Finance,* May 1981, pp. 427–39.

SAPY-MAZELLO, JEAN-PIERRE; ROBERT M. WOO; and JAMES CZECHOWICZ. *New Directions in Managing Currency Risk: Changing Corporate Strategies and Systems under FAS No. 52.* New York: Business International, 1982.

SERFASS, WILLIAM D., JR. " You Can't Outguess the Foreign Exchange Market." *Harvard Business Review,* March/April 1976, pp. 134–37.

SHAPIRO, ALAN C., and DAVID P. RUTENBERG, "Managing Exchange Risks in a Floating World." *Financial Management,* Summer 1976, pp. 48–58.

STONEHILL, ARTHUR I.; NIELS RAVN; and KARE DULLUM. "Management of Foreign Exchange Economic Exposure." In *International Financial Management*, ed. Goran Bergendahl. Stockholm: P.A. Norstedt & Soners Forlag, 1982.

TAUSSIG, RUSSELL A. "Impact of *SFAS No. 52* on the Translation of Foreign Financial Statements of Companies in Highly Inflationary Economies." *Journal of Accounting, Auditing and Finance*, Winter 1983, pp. 142–56.

WURST, CHARLES M., and RAYMOND H. ALLEMAN. "Translation Adjustments for a Strong Dollar." *Financial Executive*, June 1984, pp. 38–41.

PROBLEMS

1. Somerville Tool Company. Somerville Tool Company is filling an order from a Thai industrial company for machinery worth Bahts4,800,000. The export sale is denominated in Thai bahts and is on a one-year open account basis. The opportunity cost of funds for Somerville Tool Company is 8 percent.

The current spot rate is Baht20 per dollar, and the forward baht sells at a discount of 20 percent per annum. The finance staff of Somerville Tool Company forecasts that the baht will drop 10 percent in value over the next year. Somerville Tool Company faces the following choices:

a. Wait one year to receive the baht amount and change bahts received for dollars at that time.

b. Sell the baht proceeds of the sale forward.

c. Borrow bahts from a Bangkok bank at 28 percent per annum against the expected future receipt of the Thai importer's payment.

What do you recommend and why?

2. BMW Sports Sedan. You have just ordered a BMW sports sedan to be delivered to you in Munich, Germany, three months from today. The purchase price is DM100,000 to be paid at that time.

You have sufficient funds to buy the car. These funds are now on deposit in a U.S. savings bank, where you are earning 6 percent per annum, compounded monthly. You discover that you can open a comparable savings account at the Hofbrauhaus Savings Bank in Munich, where you can earn 8 percent per annum, compounded annually.

You want to avoid foreign exchange risk because you fear the U.S. dollar will drop in value relative to the mark over the next few months. How many dollars do you need today to pay for the BMW?

Spot rate:	DM2.6480/$.
Three-month forward rate:	DM2.6256/$.

3. Elysee, S.A. Elysee, S.A. is the Paris-based manufacturing affiliate of a U.S. corporation. Elysee's balance sheet, in thousands of French francs, is as follows:

Assets		Liabilities	
Cash	FF 3,600	Accounts payable	FF2,400
Accounts receivable	4,800	Five-year bank loan	3,600
Inventory	4,800	Capital stock	5,000
Net plant and equipment	6,000	Retained earnings	8,200
	FF19,200		FF19,200

The exchange rate between the French franc and the U.S. dollar was FF8/$. However, the French franc has just dropped in value to FF10/$. What translation loss is experienced by Elysee's U.S. parent? Explain how each account contributed to this loss.

4. Forestland, Inc. Forestland, Inc., of Los Angeles has a wholly owned subsidiary in Jungleland, whose currency is the vine, abbreviated V. The current balance sheet of the Jungleland subsidiary is given below. Note that some accounts are denominated in vines and others in dollars, but all are expressed in terms of their vine equivalent.

Assets		Liabilities	
Cash (in vines)	V 1,000	Accrued wages (in vines)	V 1,200
Cash (in dollars)	800	Short-term bank-debt (in	
A/R (in vines)	2,000	vines)	3,000
A/R (in dollars)	2,200	Long-term debt	
Inventory	2,400	(in dollars)	3,000
Net plant and equipment	4,000	Shareholders' equity	5,200
	V12,400		V12,400

Exchange rates are as follows:

Current spot rate:	V3.1250/$
Current one-year forward rate:	V4.0000/$
Forestland's forecast of the spot rate one year hence:	V5.0000/$

a. What percentage amount of devaluation of the vine does Forest-land predict?

b. What is the translation exposure created by the Jungleland subsidiary, using the current rate method?

c. What is Forestland's expected translation loss?

d. If Forestland decides to hedge its vine translation exposure in the forward exchange market, and if Forestland's corporate tax rate is 40 percent, what should Forestland do?

e. How safe is this procedure? What, for example, would be the results if one year hence the vine was traded at V3.2/$? At V6.0/$?

CHAPTER FOUR

Working Capital Management

A domestic firm can transfer cash balances freely throughout its own country without risk of loss of value. However, a multinational firm sometimes finds its cash balances tied up in a currency or country at a time when it would like to spend those funds elsewhere. These funds are either blocked or subject to substantial loss of value if moved. The major task of multinational working capital management is to unblock and/or preserve the value of these funds by managing the firm's current assets and current liabilities so that cash generated by operations is located in a currency and in a country where it is needed by the firm.

Three basic questions must be answered:

- *Goal:* Where does the firm want its liquid funds held, in terms of both country and currency?
- *Techniques:* How can liquid funds be moved from one location to another or changed from one currency into another?
- *Risk avoidance:* What should a firm do to minimize loss from future changes in the values of currencies or the freedom that is allowed to exchange one currency for another?

CONSTRAINTS ON POSITIONING FUNDS

In a purely domestic business, financial managers are generally unimpeded in their ability to locate liquid funds where they wish, primarily because all funds are in a single currency and are located in a single legal and tax jurisdiction. Expansion into the international arena creates several constraints.

Political constraints arise when sovereign governments pass laws or otherwise impede the free international flow of funds. Exchange controls are an obvious political constraint. Less obvious are confiscatory taxation of dividends and legal harassment through rules that require excessive time or fees in order to obtain necessary permits.

Tax constraints arise because of the complex interaction of tax structures in the various countries in which funds might be held. A company might find itself taxed twice on the same profit.

Transaction costs arise from bank charges for foreign exchange transactions. This constraint is sometimes aggravated by local rules that require international fund transfers to be carried out only through local banks or that preclude multilateral netting of accounts payable and receivable between affiliates owned by the same parent.

Liquidity requirements for each affiliate may limit a firm's ability to move liquid funds into a "safe" currency or location in anticipation of constraints being imposed at some future date.

A number of approaches are used to minimize the effect of constraints on positioning funds. In many respects, these approaches are unique to a particular country and firm and to a particular year. Nevertheless, some general techniques can be identified. These include:

1. Unbundling fund remittances into various kinds of financial and operational payments.
2. Tax planning when remitting funds in the form of dividends or as compensation for services rendered.
3. Adjustment of transfer prices to achieve cash positioning or tax advantages.
4. Setting up multilateral netting systems.
5. Using foreign trade zones to lessen investment in working capital.

UNBUNDLING FUND REMITTANCES

The basic purpose of an investment is to obtain a future inflow of cash, the present value of which is greater than the present value of the outflow expended to achieve that flow. Domestically, net income plus noncash charges such as depreciation are regarded as inflows because the cash represented by their sum is more or less automatically available for use elsewhere by the corporation. Net income and funds represented by noncash charges in a foreign affiliate are *not* automatically available for use by the parent corporation. Hence, financial management must plan explicitly in advance to assure that options exist by which funds may be moved to where they are needed.

Foreign cash flows can more easily be controlled if they are broken into components (that is, "unbundled") so that each cash flow is tied to specific benefits provided to the foreign affiliate. In this respect, unbundling is an adjustment to the traditional economic concept of "profit" as the total homogeneous return to owners for the combination of their investment, risk-taking, entrepreneurship, and managerial skills.

Natural cash flows within a multinational corporate network can be divided into financial flows and operational flows, as follows:

Financial Payments from Affiliate to Parent

1. Payment of Dividends to the Parent. In a domestic setting, owners are normally compensated by dividends. Such compensation combines remuneration for capital invested, risk undertaken, managerial expertise, and technological prowess into one single payment.

2. Repayment of the Principal and Interest on Intracompany Loans Made by the Parent to an Affiliate. Cash investments by a parent in its affiliate usually take the form of equity; but, in an international setting, a parent-to-affiliate loan provides a channel for a reverse cash flow because repayment of principal and interest is a valid disbursement of cash. Return of an equity investment via a liquidating dividend is likely to be discouraged or prohibited, even though the fund flows may be identical.

Operational Payments from Affiliate to Parent

1. Payment by Affiliate for Raw Materials or Manufactured Components Imported from the Parent. Most foreign affiliates are able to obtain foreign exchange to pay for imports unless the country is in the midst of a major foreign exchange crisis.

2. Payment for Use of Facilities. Buildings, aircraft, or ships may be rented or leased from the parent or a sister affiliate rather than purchased with an additional parent infusion of equity capital.

3. Payment of Royalties and License Fees. These payments are for the use of parent-owned technology, patents, or copyrights.

4. Payment for Management-Supplied Services. An affiliate must often pay for general consulting, engineering services, financial advice, or insurance coverage supplied by the parent or by sister affiliates.

Unbundling of both financial and operational payments allows the multinational corporation to move funds internationally for purposes other than general dividend remittances. Payment for items 2, 3, and 4 above could have been remitted entirely as an overhead contribution to the parent firm. However, unbundling into specific components allows both the firm and the host government a more informed view of what payments are reasonable and why they are being made.

The secret to successful unbundling is to design the venture initially so that a variety of possible conduits is created by which cash may, at some later date, be moved from affiliate to parent.

Unbundling is also useful in allocating cash returns to joint venture partners, since the partners are likely to have made different contributions. Local partners typically provide the expertise on how to operate within the foreign country, while the parent provides technological or production expertise. Either partner might be providing financial capital.

TAX ASPECTS OF UNBUNDLING

Cash moved from affiliate to parent via royalties, management fees, or other operational charges may have certain tax advantages over the use of dividends to return cash to the parent. This is because royalties and management fees are usually tax deductible in the host country, thus reducing total income taxes if the income tax rate in the host country is above the rate in the parent country. Additionally, dividend remittances from many countries are subject to a dividend withholding tax levied when dividends are remitted to foreign owners.

The situation is illustrated in the first two columns of Exhibit 4.1, in which $50,000 is remitted from affiliate to parent by dividend (column 1) or by royalty (column 2). Affiliate country income taxes are 50 percent, and parent country income taxes are 40 percent.

In Exhibit 4.1, an affiliate earns $100,000 before local income taxes and before remitting any funds to its parent. Under the

EXHIBIT 4.1 Tax Effect, Bundled and Unbundled Remittances to Parent

	Traditional (with 100 percent dividend) (1)	Unbundled (with royalty) (2)	Unbundled (royalty and dividend) (3)
Income statement of affiliate (as stated in dollars)			
1. Net income before any remittances to parent and before income taxes	$ 100.0	$ 100.0	$ 100.0
2. Less royalties and fees paid parent	0	− 50.0	− 50.0
3. Taxable income	100.0	50.0	50.0
4. Less local income taxes at 50 percent	− 50.0	− 25.0	− 25.0
5. Net after-tax income	50.0	25.0	25.0
6. Less cash dividend to parent	− 50.0	0	− 25.0
7. Retained earnings in affiliate	0	25.0	0
Income statement of parent			
8. Royalties and fees received	$ 0	$ 50.0	$ 50.0
9. Dividend received	50.0	0	25.0
10. Total received from affiliate	50.0	50.0	75.0
11. Add back foreign income tax	+ 50.0	0	25.0
12. "Grossed up" taxable income	100.0	50.0	100.0
13. Parent taxes at 40 percent	40.0	20.0	40.0
14. Less credit for foreign taxes paid	− 50.0	0	− 25.0
15. Additional taxes paid by parent	0	20.0	15.0
16. Lost income tax credit	10.0	0	0
Parent's tax and income calculation			
17. Received from affiliate (line 10)	$ 50.0	$ 50.0	$ 75.0
18. Less additional taxes paid (line 15)	0	− 20.0	− 15.0
19. Net for parent, after all taxes	50.0	30.0	60.0
20. Net reinvested in affiliate (line 7)	0	25.0	0
21. Total available, worldwide (lines 19 + 20)	$ 50.0	$ 55.0	$ 60.0

traditional approach (column 1), the firm first pays 50 percent income taxes on its pretax earnings and then remits the remaining $50,000 to its parent as a dividend. Under the unbundled approach (column 2), the firm first pays a $50,000 royalty to its parent, then pays income taxes of 50 percent on the remaining $50,000 of pretax income, and retains $25,000 for expansion of the affiliate. This $25,000 is available cash in the host country and is also a component of consolidated worldwide income as reported to shareholders. In both instances, the parent has received a total of $50,000 before calculation of parent taxes.

Financial results for the parent are shown in the middle section of Exhibit 4.1. Under the traditional approach (column 1), the parent adds back foreign tax payments to calculate a "grossed up" taxable income of $100,000. The parent then calculates home-country taxes at 40 percent of this grossed up income, or $40,000. The parent reduces this tax liability by a credit for the amount of foreign taxes already paid; in this instance, the foreign credit exceeds the home-country income tax charge, so the parent pays no additional taxes. In fact, part of the credit is lost, which is unfortunate. If the parent received dividends from another country where the tax rate was below the home-country rate, the credits could be netted. Under the unbundled approach (column 2), the parent pays a full 40 percent income tax on the royalties received.

The net result shows at the bottom of Exhibit 4.1. Lines 19 and 20 show that under the traditional approach the parent receives $50,000 after taxes and the affiliate retains nothing. The unbundled approach, line 21, shows that total retention (and thus total consolidated income) is $55,000, or $5,000 larger than under the traditional approach. However, the distribution between parent and affiliate is altered, with the affiliate now retaining a significant proportion of available cash.

Overall, then, the unbundled approach of column 2 facilitates an increase in worldwide net income and worldwide cash flow by shifting the manner in which funds are remitted and also the tax consequences of such remittances. This approach is particularly useful when the firm wants to leave funds in its foreign affiliates.

Many other combinations are possible. An additional one is shown in column 3. Had the affiliate declared a $25,000 dividend to its parent after paying royalty fees and local income taxes, the parent would have incurred additional U.S. taxes of $15,000. Net consolidated income and also net available cash would have been $60,000, all positioned in the parent country.

TRANSFER PRICING

A *transfer price* is the price at which one member of a family of firms sells to a related unit. In international business, it is the price at which the parent firm sells components or finished goods to its foreign affiliates or, alternatively, the price at which an affiliate sells to the parent.

Transfer prices are scrutinized carefully by income tax authorities worldwide. This is because the transfer price serves not only to move funds from one entity to another but also to influence the income taxes paid by both entities. The situation is illustrated in Exhibit 4.2, wherein a parent sells components to an affiliate at either a high transfer price or a low transfer price. The income tax rate in the affiliate's country is below that in the parent country.

In the above example, use of a low transfer price instead of a high transfer price has the following consequences:

1. Worldwide, consolidated, net income increases from $1,420 to $1,560.

EXHIBIT 4.2 Transfer Prices in the Multinational Firm

	High Transfer Price		Low Transfer Price	
	Parent	*Affiliate*	*Parent*	*Affiliate*
Sales price	$ 4,000	$ 5,000	$ 3,000	$ 5,000
Less cost of goods sold	− 1,000	− 4,000	− 1,000	− 3,000
Gross profit	3,000	1,000	2,000	2,000
Less operating expenses	− 800	− 500	− 800	− 500
Pretax profit	2,200	500	1,200	1,500
Less income taxes (50 percent in parent country and 36 percent in affiliate country)	− 1,100	− 180	− 600	− 540
Net profit after taxes	$ 1,100	$ 320	$ 600	$ 960
Consolidated net income	$1,420		$1,560	

2. The parent's gross profit and pretax profit decrease, result-ing in the parent alone (as a separate entity within the worldwide firm) *appearing* to be less profitable.

3. The affiliate's gross profit and pretax profit rise, resulting in an *apparent* greater profitability.

4. If the changes in apparent profitability of each separate unit identified immediately above are not understood and adjusted for, the worldwide company's internal control system will give mis-leading information. Resources may be allocated to the unit that appears more profitable, and the manager of the unit that appears less profitable may be fired! In other words, if one unit self-sacri-fices its profits for the overall benefit of the consolidated firm, that sacrifice must be considered before decisions are made based on such typical evaluation devices as return on investment, turnover, or profit margin.

5. Tax collections are reduced in the parent country, presum-ably to the unhappiness of that country's taxing authorities. Tax collections are increased in the affiliate's country.

6. Less cash is moved from affiliate to parent when the affiliate pays for its imported merchandise. Under the high transfer price policy, the affiliate sends $4,000 to the parent; whereas, under the low transfer price policy, only $3,000 is remitted.

Note that the above effects arise because of the interaction among relative tax levels and the direction in which the transfer price was changed. Opposite effects could have resulted under other combinations.

From the above example, it might appear that changes in transfer prices are an easy technique to avoid taxes or to move funds. Realistically, the range within which transfer prices may be altered is limited. Tax authorities in most countries have rules regulating how a transfer price must be set. If the actual transfer price cannot be justified, authorities will levy taxes based on what they believe the price should have been.

In the United States, Section 482 of the Internal Revenue Code generally states that transfer prices should be the same as they would have been in an "arm's-length" transaction with an unre-lated buyer. This rule does not eliminate disputes, but it does create a basis by which transfer prices can be defended or scruti-nized.

If products purchased from a related entity can also be pur-chased from an unrelated supplier, some firms use this potential outside price as the arm's-length price. Other firms use it as a reference point but allow the related parties to negotiate a price as if they were unrelated and were free to buy from an outside vendor. Still other firms use the price at which the parent sells to its unrelated commercial customers in the importing country.

The most difficult situation arises when the product or service being transferred has no outside equivalent, as when the product is a component intended for use in downstream manufacturing or when the seller possesses a patent or other proprietary right. Often, such products are priced on a cost-plus basis; however, considerable latitude exists in how cost-plus is determined. Of particular concern are the allocation of such fixed expenses as administrative overhead, selling expenses, or a share of research and development costs.

The reasonableness of transfer prices for royalties, management assistance fees, or other services is even harder to establish because of lack of outside equivalents. Many firms simply charge an amount they think is reasonable; and, if tax officials, shareholders, profit center managers, or others do not complain, the price must in fact have been "appropriate."

MULTILATERAL NETTING

A multilateral netting system enables affiliates of a multinational firm to settle their outstanding balances with each other on a net basis. Intracompany balances arise primarily from intracompany sales of goods and services and intracompany loans or other financial transactions.

A multilateral system is an expansion of a simple bilateral netting system. Assume that, at the end of a particular month, a U.S. parent owes its German affiliate deutsche marks worth $1,200,000, while simultaneously the German affiliate owes the parent $850,000. The situation can be viewed as follows:

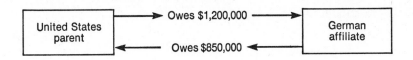

Without netting, the U.S. parent would purchase $1,200,000 worth of marks and remit them to Germany, while at the same time the German affiliate would be using $850,000 worth of marks to buy dollars to send to the United States. Total exchange transactions passing through the banking system and thus creating transaction costs paid for by the firm would be $2,050,000.

With bilateral netting, the U.S. parent would net the $850,000 due from Germany against the $1,200,000 due to Germany, and the only payment would be $350,000 sent from the United States to Germany.

A multilateral system expands this simple bilateral system with the addition of a central authority to make calculations and to either accept and disburse the net funds flows or to issue instructions as to where funds should be sent. Assume the following payments, expressed in thousands of U.S. dollars, are due:

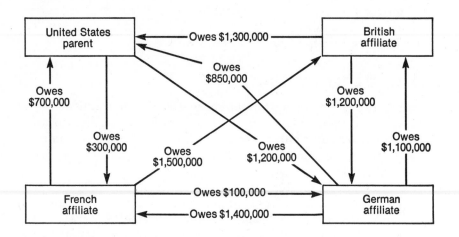

These obligations would be reported by each affiliate to the central clearing authority, which would make a calculation as follows (in thousands of dollars):

Receiving Affiliate	Paying Affiliate				Total Receipts
	United States	Britain	France	Germany	
United States	—	$1,300	$ 700	$ 850	$2,850
Britain	$ 0	—	1,500	1,100	2,600
France	300	0	—	1,400	1,700
Germany	1,200	1,200	100	—	2,500
Total payments	$1,500	$2,500	$2,300	$3,350	$9,650

The net position of each affiliate vis-à-vis all others is then calculated as follows:

	United States	Britain	France	Germany
Amount to be paid	$ 1,500,000	$ 2,500,000	$ 2,300,000	$ 3,350,000
Amount to be received	– 2,850,000	– 2,600,000	– 1,700,000	– 2,500,000
Net payment	$ – 1,350,000	$ – 100,000	$ 600,000	$ 850,000

Under a multilateral clearing system, only 4 payments totaling $2,900,000, instead of 10 payments totaling $9,650,000, need to be made:

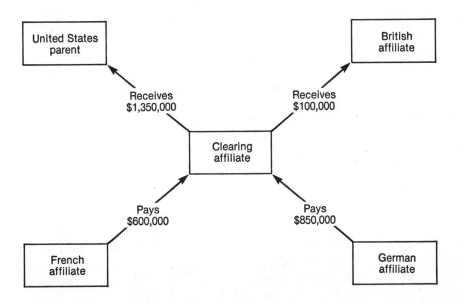

In fact, if the clearing account was located at one of the affiliates, or if the affiliates pay each other directly, one additional international payment is eliminated. In the above example, Germany could pay $750,000 to the United States and $100,000 to Great Britain, while France could pay $600,000 to the United States. Three payments would clear the net balances.

The major advantage of a multilateral netting system is a

reduction of the costs associated with a large number of separate foreign exchange transactions. These costs include both the spread between bid and ask and any charges for actual transfer of the funds—such as wire transfer fees. Another cost advantage is the reduction in float caused by fewer and smaller amounts being in transit at any given time.

The second major advantage springs from increased control over cash location provided by a central authority with both data and authority to route payments. The timing of intracompany cash flows can be set to optimize the overall firm's use of its worldwide cash resources. Established procedures for settling regularly on a prescribed monthly date also lead to greater discipline over cash management within each affiliate and to more precise near-term cash budgeting.

Multinational netting works best within a single company since only then can the worldwide enterprise exercise complete control over the timing of cash transfers. It is possible, however, to bring unrelated third-party payments into the system. For example, if a third party (an unrelated business firm) in Germany owed $100,000 to the British affiliate, that third party could be instructed to make payment in deutsche marks directly to the German affiliate, even though the third party had no direct business with the German affiliate. Such a local payment is easier for the third party and gets cash into the system quicker by reducing both mail time and float.

LEADS AND LAGS

Firms may reposition cash by *leading* or *lagging* the time at which they make operational or financial payments. All such fund transfers have a "normal" remittance date. A firm wanting to reposition cash from an affiliate to a parent, or vice versa, may accelerate the date at which the payment is made. This would be a lead. Conversely, normal payments from parent to affiliate can be lagged; that is, paid at the very last acceptable moment.

The essence of leads and lags, then, is to use variations in the timing of the transfer of funds, where the transfer will inevitably be made sooner or later. Advancing or delaying the timing of the fund transfer leaves a smaller or larger cash balance with both paying and receiving business entities.

To illustrate, suppose that the South American affiliate of a U.S. parent firm normally carries a cash balance of 800,000 escudos (E). Normal monthly sources and uses of funds for the affiliate are:

Monthly sources of funds

Cash collections from sales to local customers	E400,000
Cash collections from exports to U.S. parent	300,000
Total monthly receipt of cash	E700,000

Monthly uses of funds

Payments for wages and local raw material	E350,000
Payment for imports from U.S. parent	250,000
Local taxes	60,000
Financial payments to parent	40,000
Total monthly disbursements of cash	E700,000

The South American affiliate's cash flow is in balance in that its monthly cash receipts are equal to its monthly disbursements. In the normal course of events, its operating cash balance would remain at E800,000 except for variations caused by random fluctuations in the timing of cash receipts and disbursements within each month. The South American affiliate is also in cash flow balance with its U.S. parent in that the proceeds from exports to the United States are exactly equal to the monthly cost of imports plus dividends. (One might note that this firm would be an ideal candidate for a bilateral netting system with its U.S. parent; we will assume local regulations preclude establishment of a netting procedure.)

The affiliate's cash balance of E800,000 is equal to 800,000/700,000 = 1.14 months, or 34 days, of cash flow. Presumably, a cash balance of 34 days has been judged adequate for operational purposes. However, assume that the future value of the escudo is in doubt and the parent would like to have its affiliate reduce exposure by carrying a smaller cash balance. In order to impede a speculative flight from the escudo, exchange regulations probably prohibit any nonbusiness-related exchange of escudos for dollars, and national policy and/or a desire to avoid adverse publicity probably means that accelerating financial payments so as to move cash out of the country is unwise. Management may nevertheless decide to "work the cash balance down" by accelerating by two weeks its normal payments for imports and by decelerating by two weeks its normal collections for exports to the United States.

A two-week acceleration of foreign currency payables will re-

duce cash balances by about E125,000, and a two-week decelera-
tion of foreign currency receivables will reduce cash balances by an
additional E150,000. Both of these amounts are equal to one half of
a month's normal disbursement or receipt for that account. Under
some circumstances, a firm might be able to accelerate the timing
of its dividend disbursements, its debt repayment, or any other
business obligation; we will assume this is not possible in this
instance.

The leads and lags referred to above will together reduce the
operating cash balance by E275,000—from E800,000 down to
E525,000. This new level represents about three weeks of cash
flow. Management must decide if it is able to operate safely with
this lower level of cash.

After the initial adjustment, cash will be both collected and
disbursed on the new time schedule, with E700,000 being received
and disbursed monthly. The cash balance will stabilize at the new
level of E525,000. Foreign exchange exposure has been reduced,
but not eliminated, by the use of leads and lags and without having
to engage in any costly forward market hedges. In fact, in countries where protection is needed against a major drop in the value
of the currency, forward markets often do not exist.

Leads and lags may be used on cash settlements between a
foreign affiliate and its parent or sister affiliates or between a
foreign affiliate and nonrelated firms. The advantage of dealing
with related firms is that the timing of both receipts and payments
may be managed. With a nonrelated firm, only the timing of payments may be accelerated or decelerated. The timing of receipts is
under the control of the opposite firm, which may or may not
willingly change the time at which it remits.

FREE TRADE ZONES

A *free trade zone* is a geographic area physically within a country
but regarded as a quasi-international territory for import duty
purposes. Merchandise is often brought into a free trade zone for
holding or processing before it is finally imported into the country.
The primary advantage of a free trade zone is to reduce investment
in working capital because customs duties on imported goods are
not assessed until the goods leave the zone and actually enter the
country.

Imagine a California computer manufacturer that uses electronic devices imported from Malaysia as components. For reasons
of safety, the manufacturer needs to have two months of components on hand. Without a free trade zone, the import duty would be

paid at the time the merchandise first entered the United States—a two-month "investment" of cash. Furthermore, if 4 percent of the components proved defective after import, the firm could not recover the outlay already made for duty. In fact, the import duty would have to be paid on the shipment *before* it could be opened, inspected, and tested.

Free trade zones provide processing space where imported goods may be tested, sampled, displayed to potential customers in special exhibits, repackaged, relabeled to conform to local market requirements, used within a manufacturing process if that process is conducted in the free trade zone, or even destroyed. For example, defective imported transmissions for Volkswagon cars assembled in Pennsylvania that are damaged in shipment may be scrapped and brought into the United States as scrap metal at a much lower duty than is levied on transmissions.

In the United States, free trade zones exist in most major seaports and near a number of major airports. Additional free trade zones have been created along the U.S. border with Mexico and at such inland points as Marysville, Ohio; Smyrna, Tennessee; and MacAllen, Texas.

SUMMARY

This chapter has analyzed how multinational firms manage their cash balances, accounts receivable, and inventory internationally. The primary emphasis has been on how a firm should determine where it wants to hold its liquid cash balances and what techniques may be used to move liquid cash balances from one geographic location or currency denomination to another.

We initially looked at constraints on moving funds internationally and at the various types of financial and operational payments that constitute a normal part of operating a multinational enterprise. We then looked at the tax consequences of moving funds by dividends or by operational charges. Three specific working capital management techniques—transfer pricing, multilateral netting, and leads and lags—were next explored. The chapter closed with a look at how free trade zones can be used to preserve working capital by deferring the payment of import duties until the goods are ready to be sold.

ADDITIONAL READINGS

ANVARI, M. "Efficient Scheduling of Cross-Border Cash Transfers." *Financial Management,* Summer 1986, pp. 40–49.

BARRETT, M. EDGAR. "Case of the Tangled Transfer Price." *Harvard Business Review,* May/June 1977, pp. 20–36, 176–78.

BOKOS, WILLIAM J., and ANNE P. CLINKARD. "Multilateral Netting." *Journal of Cash Management,* June/July 1983, pp. 24–34.

BURNS, JANE V. "Transfer Pricing Decisions in U.S. Multinational Corporation." *Journal of International Business Studies,* Fall 1980, pp. 23–39.

COHEN, FRED L. "Accelerating Foreign Remittances and Collection." *Cashflow,* May 1981, pp. 36–40.

FIELCKE, NORMAN S. "Foreign Currency Positioning by U.S. Firms: Some New Evidence." *Review of Economics and Statistics,* February 1981, pp. 35–42.

FOWLER, D. J. "Transfer Prices and Profit Maximization in Multinational Enterprise Operations." *Journal of International Business Studies,* Winter 1978, pp. 9–26.

GRIFFITHS, SUSAN H. "Strategies to Upgrade Cash Management at Overseas Subsidiaries." *Cashflow,* March 1983, pp. 41–43.

JOHNSON, T. O. "International Cash Management; Slaying the Paper Tiger." *Banker,* October 1982, pp. 53–59.

KOPITS, GEORGE F. "Intrafirm Royalties Crossing Frontiers and Transfer-Pricing Behaviour." *Economic Journal,* December 1976, pp. 791–805.

MERVILLE, LARRY J., and J. WILLIAM PETTY II. "Transfer Pricing for the Multinational Firms." *Accounting Review,* October 1978, pp. 935–51.

NESS, WALTER L., JR. "U.S. Corporate Income Taxation and the Dividend Remittance Policy of Multinational Corporations." *Journal of International Business Studies,* Spring 1975, pp. 67–77.

RUTENBERG, DAVID P. "Maneuvering Liquid Assets in a Multinational Company: Formulation and Deterministic Solution Procedures." *Management Science,* June 1970, pp. B-671–84.

SHAPIRO, ALAN C. "Payments Netting in International Cash Management." *Journal of International Business Studies,* Fall 1978, pp. 51–58.

SIMPSON, H. CLAY, JR. "International Corporate Cash Management: An Introduction to the State of Current Practice." *Journal of Cash Management,* March 1982, pp. 40–44.

SRINIVASAN, VENKAT, and YONG H. KIM. "Payments Netting in International Cash Management: A Network Optimization Approach." *Journal of International Business Studies,* Summer 1986, pp. 1–20.

STONE, BERNELL K. "International versus Domestic Cash Management: The Sophistication Lag Fallacy." *Journal of Cash Management,* June/July 1983, pp. 6, 58.

PROBLEMS

1. Stalactite Mines. Stalactite Mines, a U.S. corporation is considering a $10 million investment in a foreign operation that will produce $80 million of sales revenue and $10 million of profit annually before local taxes and before any remuneration to the parent. These amounts are expected to remain constant for the next five years, after which the mine will be depleted and no assets remaining in the country will have any commercial value.

The U.S. parent may return funds to the United States only by one of two methods:

a. The foreign affiliate may declare a local currency dividend equal to 100 percent of accounting net income at the end of each year. However, exchange of the local currency amount for U.S. dollars must be delayed until the end of the fifth year. During these five years, the cash declared as dividends may be invested in local government bonds at 3 percent per annum, free of all taxes in either country. In return for this investment, the local government (which has just overthrown a dictator and needs temporary funding to get the country back on its feet) guarantees the availability of foreign exchange at the end of five years.

b. The affiliate may pay and remit to its parent at the end of each year a royalty fee equal to 4 percent of sales. If royalties are paid, however, dividends may be no greater than 40 percent of accounting net income. As before, these dividends cannot be remitted to the parent until the end of the fifth year; and, as before, they may be invested in 3 percent tax-free government bonds.

Any cash (other than that represented by dividends) remaining in the local country at the end of five years must be distributed to the miners who will be laid off when the mine expires.

Corporate tax rates are 50 percent for the affiliate and 40 percent for the U.S. parent, and the parent has a weighted-average cost of capital of 15 percent. Because of U.S. political and economic support for the new local government, the exchange rate for the local currency is expected to remain at its present rate of one-to-one with the U.S. dollar.

The parent's goal is to maximize the value of dollars received or to be received from the affiliate. Should the parent make the investment and, if it does, which method of cash recovery should be selected? Explain and show calculations.

2. Student Backpackers, Inc. Student Backpackers, Inc., (SBI) manufactures backpacks for sale on college campuses throughout the United States. Backpacks are also exported to a wholly owned distribution subsidiary in Canada. The SBI factory has an annual capacity of 6,000 backpacks, but present production is only 4,000, of which 3,000 are sold in the United States and 1,000 are sold in Canada.

Within the United States, backpacks are sold at a manufacturer's price of $15 each, a price fixed by competition and not easily raised. After-tax profit per backpack on U.S. sales is $1.50, calculated on the U.S. unit price of $15 and a production run of 4,000 as follows:

Unit sales price		$15.00
Direct labor	$3.00	
Direct material	4.50	
Manufacturing overhead	2.50	
Total manufacturing costs		10.00
Factory margin		$ 5.00
General and administrative expense		2.00
Pretax profit per unit		$ 3.00
U.S. income taxes @ 50 percent		1.50
After-tax profit per unit		$ 1.50

Direct labor consists of hourly payroll costs for plant workers, and direct material is for canvas, leather, and other raw materials. Manufacturing overhead includes both supervisory salaries and machine depreciation of $4,000 allocated on a per-unit basis. General and administrative costs are for office salaries and rent.

Student Backpackers, Inc., exports to its Canadian affiliate at a transfer price of US$11.00, derived by adding a desired profit of $1 per unit to manufacturing costs of $10. Transportation and distribution costs in Canada are equivalent to US$1 per unit, and backpacks are sold to Canadian university stores at US$15 each.

The $15 sales price in Canada was based on the following analysis of sales price elasticity and costs. A unit price of $15 and a volume of 1,000 backpacks produced the highest after-tax profits. (All prices are expressed in U.S. dollars.)

Unit price in Canada	$16.00	$15.00	$14.00	$13.00	$12.00
Import cost from United States	11.00	11.00	11.00	11.00	11.00
Transportation and distribution	1.00	1.00	1.00	1.00	1.00
Pretax unit profit	$ 4.00	$ 3.00	$ 2.00	$ 1.00	$ –0–
Less 50 percent Canadian income tax	2.00	1.50	1.00	.50	–0–
After-tax unit profit	$ 2.00	$ 1.50	$ 1.00	$ .50	$ –0–
Times Canadian unit sales volume at each price	× 700	× 1,000	× 1,400	× 2,000	× 2,500
Total profit	$1,400	$1,500	$1,400	$1,000	$ –0–

a. Assume that Student Backpackers, Inc., wants to divide per-unit profits on Canadian sales evenly between the United States and Canada so as to avoid difficulties with either tax authority. What final transfer price and selling price in Canada should the firm adopt for its Canadian business?

b. Assume that the Canadian income tax rate remains at 50 percent but the U.S. income tax rate is lowered to 30 percent. What transfer price should be adopted to minimize taxes? What policy issues are involved?

3. Pan-Continental Sellers, Inc. Pan-Continental Sellers, Inc., manufactures items in the United States, Singapore, Australia, and Norway. Production from all countries is shipped to affiliates in all other countries.

Intracompany debts (in thousands of U.S. dollars) for the current month are:

United States:	owes $300 to Singapore.
	owes $500 to Norway.
	owes $400 to Australia.
Singapore:	owes $200 to United States.
	owes $600 to Norway.
	owes $100 to Australia.
Norway:	owes $200 to United States.
	owes $100 to Singapore.
	owes $400 to Australia.
Australia:	owes $300 to United States.
	owes $300 to Singapore.
	owes $300 to Norway.

Banks charge 1 percent on all foreign exchange transactions. How should Pan-Continental settle its monthly intracompany accounts?

CHAPTER FIVE

International Sources of Funds

Access to international sources of funds gives multinational firms as well as large domestic firms with international visibility the potential for a lower cost of capital and greater availability of capital than their purely domestic counterparts. The most important international sources of funds are the Eurocurrency market and the Eurobond market. Multinational firms also often have access to national capital markets in countries in which their affiliates are located. Equity markets, particularly in the United States and the United Kingdom, have increasingly been tapped by foreign firms.

The wide array of financing sources is illustrated in Exhibit 5.1. It shows that funds may be generated internally, may be raised from other entities operating within the corporate family, and may be raised from a number of institutional sources that exist outside of the corporate family.

Sources of funds outside of the corporate family are the concern of this chapter. They include each of the several domestic capital markets in which the firm operates as well as some uniquely international institutional structures that are part of the international capital market. In this chapter, we will focus briefly on the definition of an international capital market and will then look in some detail at the Eurocurrency market, the international bond market, and the techniques by which firms finance imports and exports through the banking system.

EXHIBIT 5.1 Potential Sources of Capital for Financing a
Foreign Affiliate

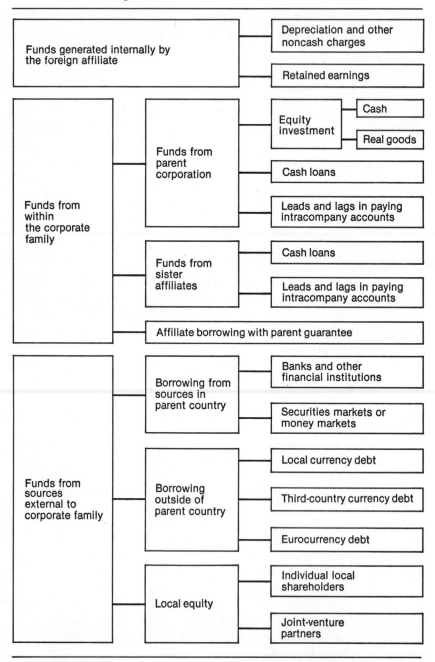

SOURCE: David K. Eiteman and Arthur I. Stonehill, *Multinational Business Finance,* 4th ed. (Reading, Mass.: Addison-Wesley Publishing, 1986), p. 457.

INTERNATIONAL CAPITAL MARKETS

An international capital market is not a physical place; it is a communications network. The commodity traded in this market is "funds": cash balances and securities in different currencies. Even more so than domestically, parties in the international capital market do not know each other, so most international capital market activity is conducted through financial intermediaries. Many of these intermediaries are the foreign divisions of the same major banks and securities firms whose names are familiar domestically; as with manufacturing firms, financial institutions have also found it necessary to go multinational in order to participate in transactions that take place outside of the United States. The financial intermediaries function in two general respects: (1) they match the needs of lenders and borrowers and (2) they substitute their own credit so that lenders and borrowers unknown to each other need not rely on the promises of any unknown opposite party but may instead depend on the reputation of the financial institution in the middle.

Most transactions in the international capital market take place in an international financial center. New York and London are the most important international financial centers. Paris, Zurich, Geneva, Amsterdam, and Tokyo are also significant players. Important "offshore" financial centers also exist in Luxembourg, Singapore, Hong Kong, the Bahamas, the Netherlands Antilles, Bahrain, Kuwait, and Panama.

International financial centers have developed historically because they are able to attract a high level of human expertise as well as physical and social infrastructures. Such centers are typically the locus of a large number of sophisticated financial institutions, such as commercial and investment (merchant) banks, insurance companies, foreign exchange dealers, and securities firms. They must possess a judicial system that is fair so that parties to any type of contract may have confidence that agreements will be consistently interpreted and enforced. Other requisites of an international financial center are highly efficient telephone, cable, and electronic communications systems, a minimum of political interference in the workings of the international economic and financial system, and a tax burden that is not troublesome.

The schematic view of an international financial center in Exhibit 5.2 depicts several types of financial transactions that might be arranged. Line A shows that the center is a major market for domestic investors and lenders providing funds to domestic users. Lines B and C show that domestic suppliers of funds often direct

---

EXHIBIT 5.2 Schematic View of Transactions in an
International Financial Center

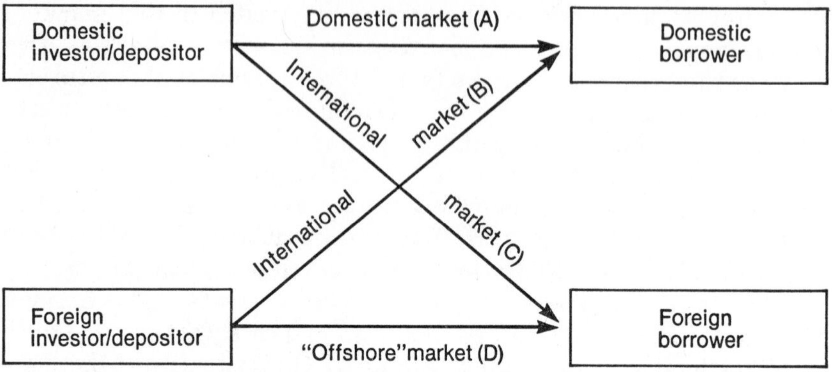

SOURCE: David K. Eiteman and Arthur I. Stonehill, *Multinational Business Finance,* 4th ed. (Reading, Mass.: Addison-Wesley Publishing, 1986), p. 384.

---

some of their funds to foreign borrowers, while foreign suppliers of funds often simultaneously place their funds in the local domestic market. In effect, international parties are drawn to participation in local financial activities because of the reputation of the market, and the distinction between local and foreign participants starts to blur. Last, line D shows that a pure "offshore" market may develop, in which foreign suppliers of funds advance capital to foreign borrowers, sometimes (but not always) by mechanisms that preclude domestic participation in the transaction.

THE EUROCURRENCY MARKET

A *Eurocurrency* is a time deposit in a bank outside the country where that currency is the official unit of account. A *Eurodollar,* the most common Eurocurrency, is thus a U.S. dollar deposited in a bank outside of the United States. Most Eurodollars are deposited in London, either with British banks, with the London branches of U.S. banks, or with banks of other countries, such as Japan, Germany, or the various countries of the Middle East. Euromarks are deutsche marks deposited in banks outside Germany, and Euro Swiss francs are Swiss francs deposited in banks outside Switzerland. Collectively, all such "offshore deposits" are known as Eurocurrencies because the market first developed in Europe. In recent years, a second locus of activity has been in the Far East, particularly Singapore, Hong Kong, and Tokyo, where the market is known as the "Asiadollar market."

The Eurocurrency and Asiadollar markets are financial intermediation markets, meaning the funds from depositors are combined by banks before being reloaned. Consequently, depositors look to their bank for recovery of their funds and do not care (and, indeed, do not know) about the ultimate disposition of those funds. Deposits in the Eurocurrency market are large, typically in increments of at least half a million U.S. dollars, and are in the form of time deposits for specific maturities on which interest is paid. Eurocurrency deposits are *not demand deposits* as that term is used in the United States.

Exhibit 5.3 shows the size of the Eurocurrency market by location, currency of denomination, and type of entity for selected dates. Although the United Kingdom (London) is the dominant center, France, Japan, and the United States are also significant centers. The rapid growth since 1981 of the U.S. Eurocurrency market is due to the introduction of *international banking facilities* (IBFs), which were first allowed in 1981. These IBFs are physically located in the United States (almost all in New York) but are treated as offshore by the regulatory and tax authorities. The motivation for permitting IBFs to exist was to enable U.S. banks to compete more cost effectively with foreign banks for the Eurocurrency business. With respect to currency of denomination, Exhibit 5.3 shows that the U.S. dollar is totally dominant, with the German mark a distant second. With reference to type of entity, the interbank market is by far the most important, representing about three quarters of the gross market size of 2 trillion dollars.

Development of the Eurocurrency Market

The modern Eurocurrency market began shortly after World War II, when the Soviet Union and other East European holders of dollars began to deposit those dollars in European banks. Strained relations with the United States made them afraid to deposit directly in U.S. banks for fear the deposits might be attached in U.S. courts by U.S. residents with claims against those governments. European banks, particularly those in London, already had limited experience before the war with dollar deposits. British bankers saw the opportunity to accept dollar deposits and make dollar loans as a way to capitalize on their centuries-old expertise in international finance at a time when their own currency was weak and subject to domestic restrictions on convertibility into other currencies.

In the 1960s, the United States responded to continued balance of payments deficits and the growing weakness of the dollar by segmenting the domestic U.S. capital market from foreign activity.

EXHIBIT 5.3 Eurocurrency Market Size (measured by foreign currency liabilities at end of period, billions of dollars)

	1976	1980	June 1983
By market center			
European centers	406	1,045	1,239
United Kingdom	201	485	635
France	50	124	127
Luxembourg	34	84	79
Belgium	20	62	74
Netherlands	21	55	52
Italy	17	46	37
Switzerland	17	35	34
Austria	—	23	25
Germany	14	25	23
Spain	7	21	17
Sweden	3	11	14
Denmark	—	3	4
Ireland	—	4	4
Unallocated	22	67	114
United States*	—	—	171
Japan	35	100	126
Canada	21	54	67
Offshore banking centers	133	325	453
Bahamas	79	126	137
Singapore	17	54	105
Bahrain	6	38	57
Hong Kong	6	32	54
Cayman Islands†	12	33	46
Panama	11	35	43
Netherlands Antilles	2	7	11
By currency of denomination			
U.S. dollar	476	1,138	1,641
German mark	70	190	175
Swiss franc	24	83	98
Japanese yen	2	17	29
British pound	6	36	25
French franc	5	22	20
Dutch guilder	5	12	20
Other currencies‡	7	26	48
By type of entity			
Nonbanks	109	327	489
Official monetary institutions	80	150	84
Other banks‡	406	1,047	1,483
Gross market size	595	1,524	2,056
Interbank liabilities within market area	281	819	1,111
Net market size	314	705	945

*International banking facilities only.

†U.S. bank branches only.

‡Includes unallocated.

SOURCE: Morgan Guaranty Trust Company of New York, *World Financial Markets,* January 1984, p. 9.

Restrictions were placed on U.S. banks and investors placing funds abroad, and, as a consequence, foreigners with dollars to invest began to place those funds in European banks.

At this time, European interest rates, including rates on Eurodollar deposits, were above U.S. domestic deposit rates, and U.S. banks were precluded by federal regulation from raising rates paid on deposits to competitive international levels. Even after the regulations were removed, however, the Euromarket continued to thrive because it had become highly efficient at accepting large-denomination deposits and relending them to borrowers at a spread that was smaller than the spread between deposit and lending rates in the United States. Political conditions, time zone differentials, different tax treatment for non-U.S. residents, and advantages in electronic communications all facilitated growth of the Eurocurrency market.

Creation of Eurodollars

The process of creating a Eurodollar is best explained with an example. Assume a Belgian firm has $10 million in a time deposit in a New York bank on which it has been earning 9 percent. The deposit is about to mature, and the Belgian firm wonders if it should redeposit the funds for another six months at 9 percent, which is still the going rate in New York.

The Belgian firm may have originally earned its dollars exporting merchandise to the United States, or indeed it may have earned the dollars exporting merchandise to Brazil, which paid in dollars. A large proportion of international trade not involving the United States is invoiced and financed with U.S. dollars. The Belgian firm wants to hold dollars rather than exchange them for Belgian francs. It may wish to import dollar-priced commodities in the future, or it may have a dollar-denominated loan to repay in several months. Interest rates on dollar deposits may be higher than rates on Belgian franc deposits after adjusting for expected changes in exchange rates.

At the time of the deposit, the balance sheets of the Belgian firm and the U.S. bank appear as follows (all dollar amounts shown in thousands):

Belgian Firm		
Time deposit in New York bank (9 percent)	10,000	

New York Bank

	Time deposit due Belgian firm (9 percent)	10,000

Step 1. The Belgian corporation learns that a London bank will pay 9.5 percent on a dollar-denominated deposit. Instead of renewing its time deposit in New York, the Belgian firm instructs the New York bank to transfer the money to the London bank, where it is placed in a six-month Eurodollar deposit account paying 9.5 percent. The New York bank transfers the deposit to a U.S. bank in which the London bank maintains a correspondent account—let us assume for simplicity that the London bank happens to maintain its correspondent account in the very same bank in which the Belgian firm had been holding dollars. Ignoring interest earned for the sake of simplicity, the several accounts would look like this after the transfer:

Belgian Firm

Time deposit in London bank (9.5 percent)	10,000	

New York Bank

	Demand deposit due London bank	10,000

London Bank

Demand deposit in New York bank	10,000	Time deposit due Belgian firm (9.5 percent)	10,000

Transfer of the dollar deposit from the New York bank to the London bank creates a Eurodollar deposit because a bank outside of the United States now has a deposit liability denominated in dollars rather than in its home currency. In six months, the London bank must return dollars plus interest to the Belgian firm.

Step 2. The London bank is temporarily holding dollar assets on which it is earning nothing while simultaneously owing dollars to the Belgian firm on which it has promised to pay 9.5 percent. Let us assume that the London bank immediately makes a dollar-denominated loan to a Spanish bank at an interest rate of 10 percent. It delivers the funds to the Spanish bank by wiring instructions to the New York bank to transfer the dollar deposit into the name of the Spanish bank. The new balance sheets would appear as follows:

New York Bank

		Demand deposit due Spanish bank	10,000

London Bank

Loan made to Spanish bank (10 percent)	10,000	Time deposit due Belgian firm (9.5 percent)	10,000

Spanish Bank

Demand deposit in New York bank	10,000	Loan due London bank (10 percent)	10,000

At the end of the day, the New York bank owes the Spanish bank, rather than the London bank, $10 million in the form of a demand deposit. The London bank has converted its New York demand deposit into a loan earning 10 percent, which is adequate to cover its interest costs of 9.5 percent; and the Spanish bank now owns the underlying demand deposit in New York, for which it is paying 10 percent.

Step 3. Eurodollar deposits are typically loaned from bank to bank in the above fashion, with each sequential bank adding a slight premium. Some borrowers in this chain are central banks, which use the acquired funds as part of their foreign exchange reserves. In our example, we will assume the final borrower in the chain is a Spanish manufacturer that wants to borrow dollars to import machine tools from the United States. Assume that the

Spanish manufacturer borrows dollars from the Spanish bank at 10.5 percent. The accounts will now be:

Spanish Bank

Loan to Spanish manufacturer (10.5 percent)	10,000	Loan due London bank (10 percent)	10,000

Spanish Manufacturer

Demand deposit in New York bank	10,000	Note payable to Spanish bank (10.5 percent)	10,000

Step 4. The Spanish manufacturer now purchases machine tools from a distributor in Illinois and pays that distributor with a check (or wire transfer) on the funds in the New York bank. As a result, the dollar demand deposit in New York is transferred to the account of the Illinois distributor. The accounts now show:

Spanish Manufacturer

Tools and equipment	10,000	Note payable to Spanish bank (10.5 percent)	10,000

Illinois Tool Distributor

Demand deposit in New York bank	10,000	Sales revenue	10,000

Step 5. The last step in the process begins when the Spanish manufacturer sells merchandise manufactured with the new tools acquired from Illinois. If the proceeds of these sales are in pesetas or any currency other than U.S. dollars, the Spanish manufacturer exchanges that currency for dollars. If the sales are in dollars, as they might be if they came from Spanish exports, dollars are acquired without a foreign exchange transaction. In either case, the Spanish manufacturer uses the acquired dollars to repay its loan plus interest to the Spanish bank. The Spanish bank, in turn, repays its loan plus interest to the London bank. The London bank, in turn, returns dollars plus interest to the Belgian firm. Thus the entire cycle unwinds, all of the Eurodollar deposits on the books of

European banks are canceled, and the final holder, the Belgian firm, receives a dollar deposit in a New York bank.

Other Possibilities. The sequence of events described above could have evolved in other directions. Any holder of Eurodollar balances could have invested them in the New York money market, in shares of common stock traded in the United States, in the U.S. real estate market, or directly in a U.S. subsidiary of a foreign firm. In all these cases, as in the original, a demand deposit in a New York (or other U.S.) bank is behind the Eurodollar transactions. Banks accepting time deposits in Eurodollars do not "create" funds or expand the money supply in the fashion described in textbooks on domestic money and banking. This is because they do not create new demand deposits in return for loans, as do domestic banks, but rather simply transfer deposits held in New York at a markup in interest rates.

One might ask why the Belgian firm did not deposit its dollars directly in the Spanish bank to earn a higher rate, or why the Spanish manufacturer did not go directly to London to borrow the dollars at the lower rate being charged there. The answer partly lies in the imperfections of international capital markets and partly in participants' different perceptions of risk. The Belgian firm probably did not know of the Spanish bank or have any easy way of finding out that a bank in Spain was paying a higher rate for Eurodollar deposits. In addition, it may simply have had more confidence in British banks—a confidence born of geographic proximity, a long history of dealing, and a desire to be a good bank client so the London bank will provide other services in the future. The Spanish bank may or may not have aggressively pursued the business of the Belgian firm. The Spanish manufacturer may be unknown in London and so unable to borrow there without first going through a long process of establishing a credit rating. If the Spanish manufacturer was unknown in London, it might have had to pay the London bank a rate higher than the rate paid to the Spanish bank.

THE INTERNATIONAL BOND MARKET

International bonds are sold to investors in countries other than the country of the borrower. There are two types of international bonds: (1) "foreign bonds" and (2) "Eurobonds." *Foreign bonds* are sold entirely within one national capital market by a syndicate of securities firms operating within that country. They are denominated in the currency of the country in which they are sold. An example would be dollar-denominated bonds issued by a Japanese trading conglomerate and sold within the United States by U.S. securities firms. Such a foreign bond issue would have to comply with the regulations of the United States. In this instance, the issue would have to be registered with the U.S. Securities and Exchange Commission. Foreign bonds sold within the United States are sometimes called *Yankee Bonds*.

By contrast, a *Eurobond* is sold to investors in a number of countries other than either the country of the issuer or the country in whose currency the bond is denominated. Eurobonds are usually underwritten by an international syndicate of securities firms and banks. If the Japanese trading conglomerate sold dollar-denominated bonds in Europe through a syndicate of British, Arab, Scandinavian, and Japanese securities firms, the issue would be a Eurobond issue. Although denominated in dollars, the issue is not subject to the legal jurisdiction of the United States and so would not have to be registered with the U.S. Securities and Exchange Commission. The issue would be subject to the jurisdiction of each country in which bonds were sold; however, since local currencies are not involved, such regulation is usually not overly restrictive. For example, securities regulations in Great Britain or Germany do not impose significant restrictions on securities purchases that are not denominated in pounds or deutsche marks, particularly when those purchases are not made by residents of Great Britain or Germany, respectively. Freedom from stringent and time-consuming regulation saves both time and money for foreign borrowers and often leads them to prefer a Eurobond offering over a foreign bond offering within a particular country.

Exhibit 5.4 presents data on international bond issues by currency during the period from 1981–84. Eurobonds denominated in U.S. dollars are the most important segment of the market. Foreign bond issues denominated in Swiss francs and sold in Switzerland are also a significant source of long-term funds.

Note that the Eurobond market is not simply a longer-maturity version of the Eurocurrency market. The Eurobond market is a direct investment market, where lenders supply funds directly to borrowers and rely on the repaying ability of those borrowers. Financial institutions arrange these placements for a commission but do not add their own credit guarantee to the process. In the Eurocurrency market, in contrast, the financial institutions provide a credit guarantee and funds are commingled so the lender does not know or care what use is actually made of the funds.

EXHIBIT 5.4 International Bond Issues by Currency (new issues with a maturity of three years or more, publicly offered or privately placed in the period, in millions of dollars)

	1981	1982	1983	1984
Eurobonds	$31,616	$51,645	$48,501	$ 79,458
U.S. dollar	26,830	43,959	38,428	63,593
German mark	1,277	2,588	3,817	4,604
British pound	501	748	1,947	3,997
Japanese yen	368	374	212	1,212
European composite units	309	1,980	2,019	3,032
Other	2,331	1,996	2,078	3,020
Foreign bonds	$21,369	$26,397	$27,822	$ 27,953
U.S. dollar	7,552	5,946	4,545	5,487
German mark	1,310	2,952	2,671	2,243
British pound	746	1,214	811	1,292
Swiss franc	8,285	11,432	14,299	12,626
Japanese yen	2,457	3,418	3,772	4,628
Other	538	1,435	1,730	1,677
Total	$52,985	$78,042	$76,323	$107,411

SOURCE: Morgan Guaranty Trust Company of New York, *World Financial Markets*, September/October 1985, p. 18.

FINANCING INTERNATIONAL TRADE

International trade is the oldest form of multinational business; as a consequence, the methods and techniques by which trade is financed have been refined over many centuries. International trade involves transit time and often involves dealing with an unknown opposite party. This is still true today in an age of jet travel and electronic communications, and it was even more true when the methods and techniques were first developed—in the days of barkentines and animal-drawn caravans. In ancient times as today, banks have been willing to finance goods in transit under a carefully structured arrangement that pinpoints at all times who bears the risk of noncompletion in the transaction.

Once exporter (seller) and importer (buyer) agree on the terms of a sale, the exporter usually wants to maintain legal title to the goods until they are paid for, or at least until payment is assured. The importer typically is reluctant to pay before the goods are shipped. Banks have developed procedures to bridge this gap of time and uncertainty and, in the process, provide the external financing needed by the trading partners.

The process involves three major documents as well as a number of others. The three major documents are:

1. Letter of credit, often abbreviated L/C.
2. Draft, sometimes called a bill of exchange.
3. Bill of lading.

Letter of Credit

A letter of credit (L/C) is a document in which a bank promises to pay a beneficiary—the exporter (seller)—for merchandise sold to the applicant—an importer (buyer). The L/C is issued after the importer applies to the bank for the L/C and satisfies the bank that it will be able to reimburse the bank for any payment the bank makes on the importer's behalf.

The essence of the L/C is a document containing the following statements:

May 9, 19—

First National Bank establishes an irrevocable letter of credit

In the favor of Exporters, Ltd., of London, United Kingdom.
For the account of Importers, Inc., of Chicago, Illinois.
Up to the sum of 8,000 U.S. dollars.

Payable by a draft drawn by Exporters, Ltd., on First National Bank, within 90 days of sight, and accompanied by the following documents:

1. Order bill of lading.
2. Customs invoice.
3. Packing list.
4. Insurance documents.

Evidencing shipment of 500 barrels of chemical solvents from London, United Kingdom, to Chicago, Illinois, United States of America.

Signed __(by bank)__

The L/C has two attributes that are particularly important. First, it gives the exporter the promise of a bank to pay, rather than a promise of the importer. Substituting the promise of a bank for that of the importer allows the exporter to rely on the promise of an established and well-known financial institution. The risk of nonpayment is diminished. In many situations, a letter of credit issued by the importer's bank will be *confirmed,* that is, guaranteed by a second bank, which is usually the bank of the exporter. In this situation, the exporter relies only on the promise of its own bank, and that bank in turn relies on the promise of the issuing bank. An L/C issued by one bank is an *unconfirmed L/C;* if the L/C is guaranteed by a second bank, it is then referred to as a *confirmed L/C.*

Second, the L/C is a mechanism by which the bank advances payment for the goods when they are shipped and is then reimbursed by the importer when the goods arrive. Having the importer's bank advance funds against subsequent reimbursement by the importer means that the merchandise can be financed during its transit time. The importer's bank is in effect extending credit to the importer by paying the exporter before the goods arrive. In fact, an application for a letter of credit is essentially an application for credit.

Letters of credit are also used in domestic trade and finance, where they are sometimes referred to as a *commercial letter of credit.* A *documentary letter of credit* is the type of L/C most often used in international trade. When a L/C is documentary, certain additional documents must be attached to any orders for payment (drafts) drawn under the terms of the L/C. Normal documents are an order bill of lading, a commercial invoice, insurance papers, and certificates of origin, analysis, or content.

These documents enable the bank to advance funds without having to verify the nature or quality of the contents. The L/C is the bank's promise to pay against *documents* stating that merchandise of certain specifications has been shipped. The bank need not verify the actual shipment, only the documents stating that the shipment has been made. If, for example, the importer wanted assurance that 50 gallon drums of a chemical had a requisite purity, the importer would have to arrange for a trusted party to physically analyze the contents and attach a certificate that the requisite purity had been met. As long as the documents are in order, the bank will pay and will expect reimbursement from the importer. Questions of quality are settled separately between seller and buyer outside of the L/C mechanism.

The Draft

A *draft* also called a *bill of exchange (B/E),* is the document by which payment is made under an L/C. A draft is an order written by the exporter (seller) instructing the bank that issued the L/C to pay because all the terms of the L/C have been complied with. The essence of the draft would be a document as follows:

June 12, 19—

To: First National Bank

Pay to the order of: *Exporters, Ltd.*

The sum of eight thousand U.S. dollars——$8,000.00

And charge to the account of Importers, Inc., under the terms of Letter of Credit No. 12345 dated May 9, 19—.

Signed   (by exporter)

The draft, along with other documents specified by the letter of credit, is presented by the exporter to its bank. The exporter's bank will either discount the draft at once, giving the exporter the face amount less a charge, or will take the draft for collection, with the cash proceeds to be advanced to the exporter at a later date. If the draft was discounted at 12 percent per annum (3 percent for three months), the exporter would receive $8,000 × 97 percent = $7,760 at once.

Drafts are of two types: *sight drafts* and *time drafts*. A sight draft must be paid by the bank that issued the L/C when it is initially presented. When a time draft is presented, the bank stamps it "accepted" and indicates that it will be paid at maturity. Such a draft is now referred to as an *acceptance* or *banker's acceptance*.

A draft drawn in accordance with the L/C illustrated above would be paid 90 days after presentation because that maturity was specified in the L/C. A commercial market exists in acceptances, so drafts that have been accepted may be sold at a discount in this market to provide funds between the date of acceptance and maturity. In other words, when a draft is accepted by a well-known bank, it becomes a negotiable instrument that may be traded in the money market at a discount, in the same fashion as negotiable certificates of deposit or commercial paper.

After the exporter presents the draft and other papers to its own bank, that bank in turn presents the draft and accompanying papers to the importer's bank. The latter either pays or promises to pay according to the terms on the L/C. If the L/C promises to pay 90 days after sight, the importer's bank simply endorses the draft to show that it has been accepted. The exporter's bank either holds this acceptance for 90 days or, if the exporter was not paid when the draft was first presented, returns it to the exporter to hold for 90 days.

When the draft is presented to the importer's bank and accepted, the bank retains the documents, including in particular the order bill of lading. The bank may now either release the order bill of lading to the importer in return for immediate payment (common practice when the draft is a sight draft) or it may release the order bill of lading to the importer in return for the importer's promise to pay in 90 days (as when the draft is a time draft). Only when in possession of the order bill of lading can the importer obtain physical possession of the goods, and this does not occur until the bank is either paid or is satisfied that the importer will pay by the time the acceptance is presented to the bank for payment.

Bill of Lading

The *bill of lading* is the third key document for financing international trade. Bills of lading are either *straight* or *to order.* A straight bill of lading instructs the carrier to deliver the goods directly to the designated consignee. The consignee does not need a copy of the bill of lading in order to receive the goods, and thus the straight bill of lading document itself is not title to the goods. A straight bill of lading is not good collateral for loans and is not normally used in conjunction with L/Cs. It is used when the merchandise has been paid for in advance, or when the transaction is being financed by the exporter, or when the shipment is to another branch or division of the same corporation.

An order bill of lading directs the carrier to deliver the goods to the order of a specified party and grants title only to the person to whom it is addressed. In conjunction with the L/C, the order bill of lading usually specifies delivery only to the order of the exporter (seller), who thus retains initial title after the goods have been shipped. The exporter endorses the order bill of lading over to its bank in return for payment or a promise to pay. The exporter's bank endorses the bill of lading over to the importer's bank in return for payment or a promise to pay. The importer's bank endorses the bill of lading over to the importer when it is paid or is satisfied that payment will be forthcoming in accordance with the arrangement between the importer and its bank. Thus, the order bill of lading eliminates the risk to the seller that the buyer will take the merchandise and then refuse to pay.

A Simplified Import Transaction

With these three basic documents, a simplified import transaction might proceed through the following steps:

1. *Basic contact and agreement.* Importer orders the goods, inquiring if the exporter will ship under a letter of credit. The exporter agrees, and relevant details (such as price, quantity, and dates of shipment) are established.
2. *Importer obtains letter of credit.* The importer goes to its own bank and obtains a letter of credit, the essence of which is that the bank guarantees that it will pay the exporter for the merchandise if the proper documents are presented. Consequently, the exporter may now ship against the promise of the bank rather than the promise of the importer.
3. *Exporter ships the merchandise on order bill of lading.* By using an order bill of lading, the exporter retains legal title to the goods, even though they are in transit.
4. *Exporter draws draft against importer's bank.* The draft is a legal order to the importer's bank to pay for the goods, based on the promise in the letter of credit. The draft is attached to the order bill of lading, which is a document of title, and sent to the importer's bank.
5. *Bank receives documents and pays exporter.* As agreed in the letter of credit, the importer's bank pays for the goods as soon as title, in the form of an order bill of lading, is given to it.
6. *Bank holds the documents until the goods arrive.* During this interval of time, the bank is financing the shipment. The bank will charge interest for this time interval.
7. *Goods arrive.* The bank collects funds from the importer and releases the order bill of lading so that the importer can take physical possession.

The above sequence is only one of many variations, most of which are more complicated. However, the above sequence illustrates the major steps in the process.

SUMMARY

This chapter looked at international sources of funds. For short-term needs, firms may borrow in the Eurocurrency market or, if they have excess liquidity, they may decide to invest in a Eurocurrency deposit. For longer-term needs, many multinational and large domestic corporations sell bonds in the longer-term international bond market. Import and export of goods and services can be financed through the banking system, using letters of credit, drafts, and order bills of lading. The purpose is to obtain funds while goods are in transit and with a minimum of risk of nonpayment.

ADDITIONAL READINGS

ALLAN, IAIN. "Return and Risk in International Capital Markets." *Columbia Journal of World Business*, Summer 1982, pp. 3–23.

CELI, LOUIS J., and I. JAMES CZECHOWICZ. *Export Financing, A Handbook of Sources and Techniques*. Morristown, N.J.: Financial Executives Research Foundation, 1985.

DUFEY, GUNTER, and IAN H. GIDDY. "Innovation in the International Financial Markets." *Journal of International Business Studies*, Fall 1981, pp. 33–51.

FOLKS, WILLIAM R., and RAMESH AVANTI. "Raising Funds with Foreign Currency." *Financial Executive*, February 1980, pp. 44–49.

FRYDL, EDWARD J. "The Eurodollar Conundrum." *Federal Reserve Bank of New York Quarterly Review*, Spring 1982, pp. 11–19.

HAWAWINI, GABRIEL. *European Equity Markets: Price Behavior and Efficiency*. New York: New York University, Salomon Brothers Center, Monograph 1984–4/5.

HODJERA, ZORAN. "The Asian Currency Market: Singapore as a Regional Financial Center." *IMF Staff Papers*, June 1978, pp. 221–53.

JENSEN, FREDERICK H., and PATRICK M. PARKINSON. "Recent Developments in the Bankers Acceptance Market." *Federal Reserve Bulletin*, January 1986, pp. 1–12.

KIDWELL, DAVID S.; M. WAYNE MARR; and G. RODNEY THOMPSON. "Eurodollar Bonds: Alternative Financing for U.S. Companies." *Financial Management,* Winter 1985, pp. 18–27.

LEES, FRANCIS A., and MAXIMO ENG. "Developing Country Access to the International Capital Markets." *Columbia Journal of World Business,* Fall 1979, pp. 71–84.

LOGUE, DENNIS E., and LEMMA W. SENBET. "External Currency Market Equilibrium and Its Implications for Regulation of the Eurocurrency Market." *Journal of Finance,* May 1983, pp. 435–47.

PARK, Y. S. "The Economics of Offshore Financial Centers." *Columbia Journal of World Business,* Winter 1982, pp. 31–35.

QUINN, BRIAN S. "The International Bond Market for the U.S. Investor." *Columbia Journal of World Business,* Fall 1979, pp. 85–90.

YASSUKOVICH, S. M. "Eurobonds and Debt Rescheduling." *Euromoney,* January 1982, pp. 60–62.

PROBLEMS

1. Eurodollars and Asiadollars. The following banking transactions take place. Record the various transactions in the T-accounts shown below, assuming all transactions are effected by wire and thus occur on the same day. (Consequently, no interest obligations need to be recorded.) When completed, calculate the total amount of offshore dollar deposits, both Eurodollars and Asiadollars, recorded on the books of both non-U.S. banks and U.S. banks.

Transactions:

1. Lloyds Bank, London, accepts a US$500,000 deposit for one year, agreeing to pay 8 percent interest. The funds are received in the form of a dollar deposit at their New York correspondent, Chemical Bank.

2. Seven Sisters Petroleum, a global oil exploration firm, (*a*) borrows $500,000 for one year from Lloyds Bank at 8¼ percent interest. Seven Sisters receives the funds in the form of a dollar deposit at Chemical Bank. Seven Sisters then (*b*) uses the funds to purchase an oil-drilling rig from Pandan Valley Tool Company, Singapore. Seven Sisters (*c*) pays Pandan Valley $500,000 by transferring its deposit at Chemical to Pandan Valley.

3. Pandan Valley Tool Company (*a*) deposits the $500,000 in a U.S. dollar account in Overseas Chinese Banking Corporation (OCBC), Singapore. OCBC (*b*) keeps its dollar balances with its New York correspondent, Chemical Bank.

4. OCBC (*a*) loans $500,000 for one year at 8.5 percent interest to Wooden Shoe Radio Corporation of Amsterdam, which (*b*) uses the $500,000 to pay for purchases of radios from Keng Luan Electronics of Penang. Keng Luan Electronics (*c*) deposits the $500,000 received from Wooden Shoe in its dollar account with Chemical Bank in New York.

Chemical Bank, New York

Lloyds Bank, London

Seven Sisters Petroleum

Pandan Valley Tool Company, Singapore

Overseas Chinese Banking Corporation, Singapore

Wooden Shoe Radio, Amsterdam

Keng Luan Electronics, Penang

2. Villa Trading Company. Villa Trading Company has received an order for merchandise to be exported to Australia under the terms of a letter of credit issued by Koala Banking Corporation on behalf of an Australian importer. The letter of credit specifies that the face value of the shipment, US$5 million, will be paid nine months after Koala "accepts" a draft drawn by Villa in accordance with the terms of the letter of credit. The current discount rate on nine-month acceptances is 12 percent per annum, and Villa's weighted-average cost of capital is 16 percent.

Villa wonders how much cash it can expect from the sale if it holds the acceptance until maturity. Alternatively, Villa wonders if it should sell the acceptance at once at a discount in the money market.

CHAPTER SIX

Cost of Capital and Financial Structure

A firm's cost of capital can be lowered and its availability of capital increased by following a strategy by which it gains access to international money and capital markets. Such a strategy increases the firm's ability to attract foreign investors, reduces the negative effects of market segmentation, enables investors to satisfy their international portfolio diversification motive, and might reduce the firm's foreign exchange risk through diversification. A firm's optimal financial structure can also be influenced by such a strategy.

AVAILABILITY OF CAPITAL

A firm can lower its marginal cost of capital by gaining access to the Eurocurrency market, the Eurobond market, and foreign domestic bond and equity markets. This is because the firm can escape limitations on capital availability in its home market. Even the largest firms can only raise a finite amount of debt or equity in their domestic markets in the short run. For example, IBM might be able to sell a $1 billion new bond issue to U.S. investors at some point during the year, even though it is competing with other private-sector bond issuers and the U.S. Treasury for the same pool of savings. If IBM tried to sell a $2 billion bond issue at one time, however, it would probably not be able to do so at a reasonable yield because the market demand would be saturated for that par ticular type of security and the underwriters would be afraid to take on the risk of sitting with unsold IBM bonds. On the other

EXHIBIT 6.1   Availability of Funds and the Cost of Capital

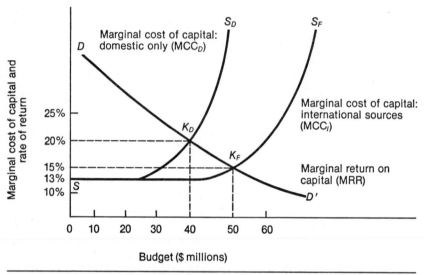

SOURCE: David Eiteman and Arthur Stonehill, *Multinational Business Finance*, 4th ed. (Reading, Mass.: Addison-Wesley Publishing, 1986), p. 426.

hand, it might be feasible for IBM to combine a $1 billion bond sale to U.S. investors with a $1 billion bond sale to foreign investors in the Eurobond market. IBM would be tapping two different pools of savings rather than one pool. The same reasoning for use of foreign capital markets applies to short-term borrowing in the Eurocurrency market and even to equity issues in foreign capital markets.

Exhibit 6.1 illustrates how gaining access to foreign sources of funds reduces the marginal cost of capital and thereby increases the desirable size of the capital budget (i.e., more projects can be profitably accepted for investment). The line DD' represents the marginal rate of return on capital. This is calculated by ranking all potential projects according to expected internal rate of return. The curve SS_D represents the increasing marginal cost of capital as the firm expands its capital budget. The more funds needed in the short run, the more expensive the cost of those funds. The marginal cost of capital curve becomes very steep once the domestic capital market has been tapped for all the less expensive sources of funds, for from then on the firm must utilize more expensive sources, such as not taking discounts on purchases or raising new equity funds. The optimal budget in the domestic case is $40 million—the point K_D, where the marginal cost of capital intersects the marginal return on capital. The firm's marginal cost of capital at that point is 20 percent.

If the firm is able to raise part of its capital in foreign markets, its marginal cost of capital schedule would be flattened and appear as the curve SS_F. In this case, the firm would utilize not only the least expensive sources of domestic capital but also similar sources abroad. For example, in the IBM case, IBM could sell both domestic bond and Eurobond issues. With access to foreign capital markets, the new optimal capital budget becomes $50 million (the point K_F). The new marginal cost of capital would be 15 percent compared to 20 percent in the domestic case.

The lower marginal cost of capital in Exhibit 6.1 could also result from increased access to foreign equity investors. Many firms list on foreign stock exchanges to make their stock more easily available to foreign investors. In recent years, it has also become more common to sell new issues of equity to foreign investors. This has been particularly attractive to foreign firms residing in countries that have illiquid equity markets. For example, since 1981, at least five Scandinavian firms have raised significant amounts of equity in the U.S. capital market through SEC-registered public issues.[1] In addition, numerous foreign firms have raised equity in the U.K. market and listed on the London Stock Exchange.

MARKET SEGMENTATION

If a firm has no choice but to raise all of its capital in an illiquid and segmented domestic capital market, it will probably experience a higher cost of capital than a firm with access to international capital markets. A capital market is said to be *segmented* if securities in that market are mispriced by international standards even if they are correctly priced by the standards of its domestic market. In a typical case, the required rate of return on the common stock of a firm restricted to its segmented domestic market

---

[1]The five Scandinavian firms are Novo Industri A/S (Denmark), L.M. Ericsson Telephone Company (Sweden), AB Fortia (Sweden), Norsk Data A/S (Norway), and Gambro AB (Sweden). All five of these firms are registered with the U.S. Securities and Exchange Commission. For a detailed description of the U.S. equity issue in 1981 by Novo Industri A/S, see Arthur Stonehill and Kåre Dullum, *Internationalizing the Cost of Capital in Theory and Practice: The Novo Experience and National Policy Implications* (Copenhagen: Nyt Nordisk Forlag Arnold Busck, 1982; and New York: John Wiley & Sons, 1982)

would be higher than that required by investors resident in other capital markets.

Causes of Market Segmentation

A domestic capital market may exist segmented from world capital markets because of government interference or because of foreign investors' perceptions. A government can purposely, or even inadvertently, segment its capital market by imposing taxes on security transactions, by restricting foreign exchange transfer or convertibility, or by interfering with the free functioning of its capital market. Even without government interference, however, a market can be segmented because investors from other countries are not able to obtain enough information on securities in that market. Information barriers arise from language differences, lack of appropriate disclosure, or unfamiliarity with investment institutions in that market. Foreign investors may also cause a domestic market to remain segmented because they perceive the domestic market to have too much foreign exchange and political risk.

It should be noted that a market may be segmented and yet be efficient in a finance theory context. A market is defined as *efficient* if security prices in that market are based on all available information and if any new information is quickly captured in those security prices. Even though security prices in a segmented market might reflect all information available to domestic investors (who comprise the whole market), foreign investors would not be participants in this price-setting activity. Therefore, prices set in this manner would reflect domestic preferences but not international preferences.

The Marginal Cost of Capital:
Segmented versus Integrated Markets

Even if the home market of a firm is segmented, that firm may be able to shed the limitations of its home market by aggressively exposing its securities to international investors. In this manner, it may achieve an international pricing of its securities rather than being limited to domestic pricing. In other words, the firm would hope that an efficient world market would award the firm a higher price for its common stock and bonds than the efficient domestic market is willing to award. Indeed, this was the main motivation for the aforementioned five Scandinavian firms to sell equity in the U.S. market in the 1980s.

Exhibit 6.2 illustrates how the marginal cost of a firm's capital

EXHIBIT 6.2 Market Segmentation and the Cost of Capital

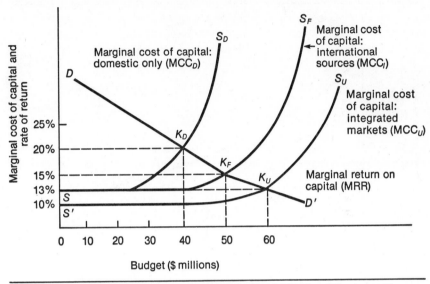

SOURCE: David Eiteman and Arthur Stonehill, *Multinational Business Finance,* 4th ed. (Reading, Mass.: Addison-Wesley Publishing, 1986), p. 430.

can be reduced and its capital budget expanded by sourcing its funds in an integrated world market. Using the same example as in Exhibit 6.1, the curve $S'S_U$ represents the new marginal cost of capital schedule, where the cost of capital is 13 percent and the capital budget is $60 million. At this intersection (K_U), the firm captures the entire benefit of both the expanded availability of funds and the removal of the market segmentation.

INTERNATIONAL PORTFOLIO DIVERSIFICATION

Ever since portfolio theory was first introduced in 1959, investors have had a solid theoretical basis for diversifying their holdings of securities and other assets. The object of diversification is to minimize the risk of a portfolio for a given rate of return or, conversely, to maximize the portfolio's rate of return for a given level of portfolio risk.

Exhibit 6.3 shows the traditional diagram used to illustrate the advantage of portfolio diversification in the domestic case. As the investor or portfolio manager increases the number of securities in a portfolio, the risk of that portfolio diminishes—up to a point. In this diagram, nearly all of the risk reduction is achieved after 30

EXHIBIT 6.3   Risk Reduction through Diversification:
The Domestic Case

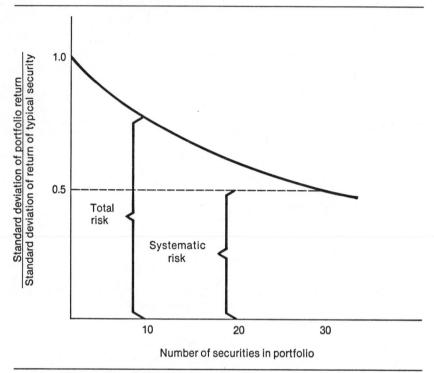

Number of securities in portfolio

SOURCE: Donald R. Lessard, "International Diversification and Direct Foreign Investment," in *Multinational Business Finance,* 4th ed., ed. David Eiteman and Arthur Stonehill (Reading, Mass.: Addison-Wesley Publishing, 1986), p. 275.

securities have been included in the portfolio. If the returns on these individual securities are not perfectly correlated with one another, random fluctuations in returns for each security would tend to be offset by random fluctuations in returns for the other securities. Therefore, diversification eliminates what is called the *unsystematic risk* of the portfolio.

Why does risk reduction virtually stop after 30 securities are added to the portfolio? The reason is that the returns on all securities in the domestic market are affected to varying degrees by the overall movement of that market. Thus, all stock prices in the United States tend to move up and down to some extent with the overall U.S. stock market. This tendency to move with the market is called *systematic risk.* It cannot be eliminated by further domestic diversification.

In the 1960s, finance theorists extended portfolio theory to the

---

EXHIBIT 6.4   Risk Reduction through National and
International Diversification

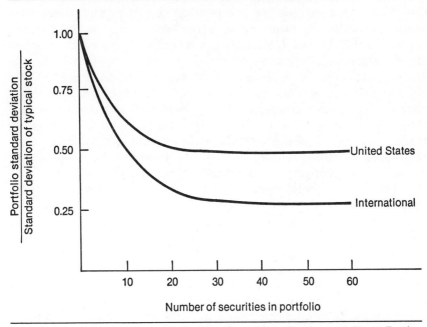

Number of securities in portfolio

SOURCE: Donald R. Lessard, "International Diversification and Direct Foreign Investment," in *Multinational Business Finance*, 4th ed., ed. David Eiteman and Arthur Stonehill (Reading, Mass.: Addison-Wesley Publishing, 1986), p. 276.

international case. This is depicted in Exhibit 6.4. As foreign securities are added to a domestic U.S. portfolio, its risk is reduced below that of the portfolio containing only U.S. securities. The reason is that returns on foreign securities are also random but not necessarily influenced by the U.S. stock market. Therefore, the systematic risk of an international portfolio can be reduced below that of a purely U.S. domestic portfolio. Even in the internationally diversified portfolio, however, some systematic risk remains because there is some degree of correlation between securities prices worldwide. The more world markets become integrated, the more closely returns on securities tend to be correlated and the less the benefit of international portfolio diversification.

How can a business firm benefit from the desire of investors to diversify their portfolios internationally? One answer is for the firm to make sure that its stock can readily be purchased and sold by foreign investors. For example, suppose that a U.S. pension fund manager wants to hold an internationally diversified portfolio to gain the benefits described above. That manager must find enough investment-grade foreign stocks (or bonds). Perhaps the returns on Scandinavian stocks are not correlated with the U.S. market and, therefore, are desirable for the pension fund's portfolio. An easy solution would be for the portfolio manager to buy one or more of the Scandinavian stocks that are registered with the SEC, listed on an organized U.S. exchange, or at least traded over the counter and widely followed by U.S. security analysts. The stock prices of these Scandinavian companies should increase because of the demand by such U.S. portfolio managers. Other Scandinavian stocks, even if they are of comparable quality, would not be so visible or easily traded. The prices of those stocks would probably not benefit from this international demand and would therefore continue to be priced lower according to Scandinavian norms.

U.S. firms can also benefit by becoming more visible to foreign investors. Non-U.S. investors also seek the gains from diversifying internationally. For example, in recent years, Japanese investors have been heavy investors in foreign stocks and bonds, and Japanese stocks have been eagerly sought by portfolio managers in other countries.

The overall potential for international diversification is difficult to measure because even stocks that are not easily available internationally can be purchased in their domestic stock markets. As investors become more sophisticated, diversification becomes increasingly likely, with the result that world markets are becoming more integrated. Exhibit 6.5 is an attempt to measure the total world market for both stocks and bonds in 1980. Note the dominant size of the U.S. market for both stocks and bonds. Exhibit 6.6 attempts to measure the market value of non-U.S. stocks. The non-U.S. stocks are dominated by Japan and the United Kingdom, with Canada, Germany, and Australia of some significance.

Exhibit 6.7 measures the average annual percentage returns on stocks by country during the period from 1960–80. The Asian stocks, namely Hong Kong, Japan, and Singapore, had by far the best annual rates of return. As you would expect, they also had the highest risk, as measured by the standard deviation of their returns. However, that riskiness could have been virtually eliminated if those stocks were held in internationally diversified portfolios; while in retrospect, the returns on those portfolios would have been increased by the high rates of return on the Asian stocks.

Some financial theorists believe that multinational firms benefit from the international portfolio diversification motive of investors. If investors cannot find enough suitable foreign stock, their

EXHIBIT 6.5 Size of World Equity and Bond Markets at the End of 1980 in Billions of U.S. Dollars (World total = $5,289.9 billion)

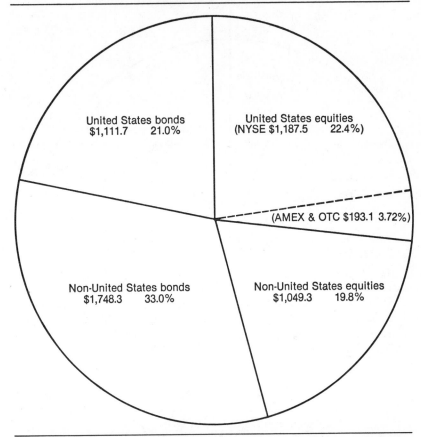

United States bonds
$1,111.7   21.0%

United States equities
(NYSE $1,187.5   22.4%)

(AMEX & OTC $193.1 3.72%)

Non-United States bonds
$1,748.3   33.0%

Non-United States equities
$1,049.3   19.8%

SOURCE: Roger C. Ibbotson, Richard C. Carr, and Anthony W. Robinson, "International Equity and Bond Returns," originally published in the *Financial Analysts Journal*, July–August 1982, but abridged and reprinted in *International Financial Management*, 2nd ed., Donald R. Lessard, ed. (New York: John Wiley & Sons, 1985), p. 32.

theory suggests that investors might pay a premium to hold the stocks of multinational firms as a proxy for international diversification. Although the multinational firms may not be internationally diversified in an optimal way from the investors' viewpoint, they do provide a second-best alternative. Furthermore, the investor achieves some international diversification of business risk and foreign exchange risk by investing in multinational firms.

EXHIBIT 6.6   Market Values of Non-U.S. Equities at the
End of 1980 in Billions of U.S. Dollars
(Non-U.S. equity total = $1,049.3 billion)

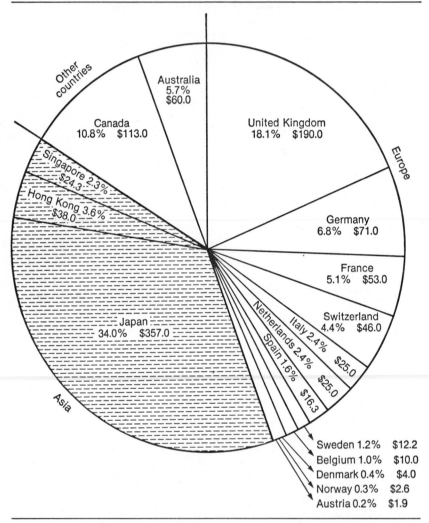

SOURCE: Roger C. Ibbotson, Richard C. Carr, and Anthony W. Robinson, "International Equity and Bond Returns," originally published in the *Financial Analysts Journal*, July–August 1982, but abridged and reprinted in *International Financial Management*, 2nd ed., Donald R. Lessard, ed. (New York: John Wiley & Sons, 1985), p. 33.

EXHIBIT 6.7   World Equities: Summary Statistics, 1960–1980

| Asset | 1980 Year-End Value in | Annual Returns in U.S. Dollars | | | Index 1959 = 1.00 | Year-End Wealth Billions U.S. $ |
		Compound Return (%)	Arithmetic Mean (%)	Standard Deviation (%)		
Non-U.S. equities						
Europe						
Austria		9.1%	10.3%	16.9%	6.23	$ 1.9
Belgium		9.2	10.1	13.8	6.39	10.0
Denmark		9.5	11.4	24.2	6.72	4.0
France		6.2	8.1	21.4	3.56	53.0
Germany		8.3	10.1	19.9	5.32	71.0
Italy		2.4	5.6	27.2	1.63	25.0
Netherlands		9.3	10.7	17.8	6.45	25.0
Norway		10.3	17.4	49.0	7.81	2.6
Spain		8.4	10.4	19.8	5.49	16.3
Sweden		8.4	9.7	16.7	5.40	12.2
Switzerland		10.2	12.5	22.9	7.74	46.0
United Kingdom		10.0	14.7	33.6	7.39	190.0
Europe total		8.4	9.6	16.2	5.47	$ 457.0
Asia						
Hong Kong*		24.6	40.3	61.3	11.24	$ 38.0
Japan		15.6	19.0	31.4	20.86	357.0
Singapore*		23.2	37.0	66.1	9.96	24.3
Asia total		15.9	19.7	33.0	22.29	$ 419.3
Other						
Australia		9.8	12.2	22.8	7.12	$ 60.0
Canada		10.7	12.1	17.5	8.47	113.0
Other total		10.6	11.9	17.1	8.24	$ 173.0
Non-U.S. total equities		10.6	11.8	16.3	8.23	$1,049.3
U.S. total equities		8.7	10.2	17.7	5.78	$1,380.6
World total equities		9.3	10.5	15.8	6.47	$2,429.9

SOURCE: Roger C. Ibbotson, Richard C. Carr, and Anthony W. Robinson, "International Equity and Bond Returns," originally published in the *Financial Analysts Journal*, July–August 1982, but abridged and reprinted in *International Financial Management*, 2nd ed., Donald R. Lessard, ed. (New York: John Wiley & Sons, 1985), p. 34.
*1970–1980

FOREIGN EXCHANGE RISK

Foreign exchange risk influences a firm's cost of capital in a number of ways. On the one hand, foreign exchange risk increases the uncertainty of a multinational firm's cash flows, with a resulting negative effect on its cost of capital. On the other hand, as we have discussed earlier, diversifying operations and financing internationally has advantages in managing foreign exchange economic exposure.

Foreign exchange risk is a particularly important consideration in choosing where to raise debt. We have described earlier the international Fisher effect, which holds that, in equilibrium, exchange rate changes should just offset differences in interest rates between two countries. If the international Fisher effect is true, of course, which currency a firm borrows or an investor holds is irrelevant. Needless to say, this relationship does not always hold true, so it does make a difference. Some multinational firms have learned this the hard way.

At times, some U.S. multinational firms have been lured by low interest rates to borrow long term in a foreign currency. For example, a firm may be tempted to borrow in Swiss francs because Swiss interest rates are lower than U.S. rates. Assume that General Motors decides to borrow Swiss francs for 10 years at a 4 percent annual interest rate instead of U.S. dollars at a 10 percent interest rate. GM believes the Swiss franc will appreciate only 3 percent per year vis-à-vis the U.S. dollar. The dollar cost of this debt before tax can be calculated as follows:

$$\text{Cost of debt equals} \begin{bmatrix} \text{Principal and interest} & \text{times} & \text{Exchange rate change} \end{bmatrix} \text{minus Principal} \quad \text{times 100}$$

$$K = \{[(1.04) \times (1.03)] - 1.00\} \times 100 = 7.12 \text{ percent.}$$

This would be almost 3 percent less than borrowing in U.S. dollars. Of course, General Motors might have guessed wrong, and the Swiss franc might appreciate by 7 percent per year, for example. In that case, the cost of debt would be 11.28 percent, or over 1 percent more expensive than in dollars. If the international Fisher effect holds, the Swiss franc should appreciate by 5.7692 percent, that is, $1.04 \times 1.057692 = 1.10$, in order to be indifferent between the two alternatives.

OPTIMAL FINANCIAL STRUCTURE

Multinational firms may be able to support higher debt ratios than their domestic counterparts because the cash flows of multinational firms are naturally diversified by currency and geographic area. If returns are not perfectly correlated between countries, the multinational firm might achieve the same type of reduction of unsystematic risk on its portfolio of projects as an investor achieves on a portfolio of securities. For example, a firm's subsidiary in France might be generating healthy income and cash inflows thanks to a booming French economy, while its subsidiary in Mexico is suffering losses and cash outflow because of a Mexican recession. Thus, if business risk is reduced through international diversification, a firm could support a higher level of financial risk, that is, a higher debt ratio.

The optimal financial structure of a multinational firm may be somewhat influenced by the needs of its foreign subsidiaries. Local borrowing in a foreign currency may be needed as a balance sheet hedge to manage foreign exchange risk in individual subsidiaries. Local borrowing may also be motivated by a desire to reduce political risk or to minimize worldwide taxes.

In joint ventures, the appropriate financial structure may depend on what is considered normal in the host country of the joint venture partner. Finance structure norms vary considerably by country. Exhibit 6.8 presents a survey of debt ratio norms for a selected group of countries. Note that the debt ratio norms for all countries in the survey are higher than in the United States, with Japan having the highest debt ratio norm.

Even if the multinational firm has 100 percent ownership of its foreign subsidiary, it may sometimes be appropriate for cosmetic reasons to maintain a debt ratio that is consistent with local norms. This might mute local criticism that the foreign-owned firm has either too little or too much debt compared to local competitors. On the other hand, the overall debt ratio of the consolidated multinational firm should not be distorted just to satisfy local concerns. After all, the overall debt ratio should be the one appropriate for the main capital market or markets in which the firm raises its funds. A U.S. firm should maintain an overall debt ratio appropriate for the U.S. capital market, and a Japanese firm should maintain an overall debt ratio appropriate for the Japanese market. It is, nevertheless, interesting to note from Exhibit 6.8 that appropriate debt ratios do vary considerably by country and, to some extent, by industry within a country.

EXHIBIT 6.8 Debt Ratios in Selected Industries and Countries, 1979–1980*

	Alcoholic Beverages	Auto-mobiles	Chemicals	Electrical	Foods	Iron and Steel	Nonferrous Metals	Paper	Textiles	Total
Benelux	41.4	61.8	60.0	50.8	64.3	66.2	41.4	63.2	54.2	55.9
France	56.3	67.3	72.1	72.5	77.7	74.1	66.3	74.4	73.9	70.5
West Germany	—	57.1	56.2	66.4	48.8	51.6	67.8	69.8	65.0	60.3
Italy	—	21.7	67.7	79.2	83.4	90.2	86.1	77.4	77.7	72.9
Japan	—	71.3	81.2	65.7	76.3	87.5	88.2	76.6	77.6	78.1
Sweden	79.1	75.2	67.5	76.9	62.8	69.3	56.1	55.5	59.7	66.9
Switzerland	—	—	—	63.2	53.7	63.8	—	—	—	60.2
United Kingdom	41.9	72.8	49.8	59.9	55.3	50.7	56.7	55.9	50.7	54.9
United States	51.1	58.0	54.7	53.6	55.4	54.3	57.6	58.2	47.5	54.5
Total	54.0	60.7	63.7	65.4	64.2	67.5	65.0	66.4	63.3	

SOURCE: J. Markham Collins and William S. Sekely, "The Relationship of Headquarters' Country and Industry Classification to Financial Structure," *Financial Management*, Autumn 1983, p. 48.

*Debt ratio = Total debt/Total assets at book value.

SUMMARY

Access to foreign sources of capital enables a firm to increase its availability of capital and to lower its marginal cost of capital compared to sourcing all funds in the domestic market. Firms located in a segmented home capital market can also lower their marginal cost of capital still further by making their equity and debt more visible and available to foreign investors. Their objective is to gain an international pricing standard for their securities rather than being limited to their domestic market's standard.

International portfolio diversification allows an investor to achieve a higher rate of portfolio return for a given level of risk or a lower risk for a given rate of return. Business firms can benefit from the desire by investors to hold foreign securities for purposes of diversification by making their stock easily available to foreign investors.

Multinational firms are subject to foreign exchange risk, a fact that might normally increase their cost of capital. However, these firms are diversified by both currency and geographic operations. Such diversification reduces the firm's risk in the same manner as portfolio investors reduce their risk through diversification. As a result, foreign exchange risk may not increase the cost of capital for a multinational firm.

A multinational firm's optimal financial structure may be affected by its international sourcing of capital. In some cases, the firms borrow in local currencies for reasons related to reducing foreign exchange risk, political risk, and taxation. If a joint venture is involved, the joint venture's financial structure may be determined by local norms. Such norms vary widely among countries.

ADDITIONAL READINGS

ADLER, MICHAEL, and BERNARD DUMAS. "International Portfolio Choice and Corporation Finance: A Synthesis." *Journal of Finance,* June 1983, pp. 925–84.

AGMON, TAMIR, and DONALD LESSARD. "Investor Recognition of Corporate International Diversification." *Journal of Finance,* September 1977, pp. 1049–55.

BIGER, NAHUM. "Exchange Risk Implications of International Portfolio Diversification." *Journal of International Business Studies,* Fall 1979, pp. 64–74.

CHOI, FREDERICK D. S., and ARTHUR STONEHILL. "Foreign Access to U.S. Securities Markets: The Theory, Myth and Reality of Regulatory Barriers." *The Investment Analyst,* July 1982, pp. 17–26.

COHN, RICHARD A., and JOHN J. PRINGLE. "Imperfections in International Financial Markets: Implications for Risk Premia and the Cost of Capital to Firms." *Journal of Finance,* March 1973, pp. 59–66.

COLLINS, J. MARKHAM, and WILLIAM S. SEKELY. "The Relationship of Headquarters' Country and Industry Classification to Financial Structure." *Financial Management,* Autumn 1983, pp. 45–51.

EAKER, MARK R. "Denomination Decisions for Multinational Transactions." *Financial Management,* Autumn 1980, pp. 23–29.

ERRUNZA, VIHANG R., and ETIENNE LOSQ. "International Asset Pricing under Mild Segmentation: Theory and Test." *Journal of Finance,* March 1985, pp. 105–24.

ERRUNZA, VIHANG R., and LEMMA W. SENBET. "The Effects of International Operations on the Market Value of the Firm: Theory and Evidence." *Journal of Finance,* May 1981, pp. 401–17.

ERRUNZA, VIHANG R. and LEMMA W. SENBET. "International Corporate Diversification, Market Valuation, and Size-Adjusted Evidence." *Journal of Finance,* December 1984, pp. 1311–24.

EUN, CHEOL S., and BRUCE G. RESNICK. "Estimating the Correlation Structure of International Share Prices." *Journal of Finance,* December 1984, pp. 1311–24.

FATEMI, ALI M. "Shareholder Benefits from Corporate International Diversification." *Journal of Finance,* December 1984, pp. 1325–44.

GRUBEL, HERBERT G. "Internationally Diversified Portfolios: Welfare Gains and Capital Flows." *American Economic Review,* December 1968, pp. 1299–1314.

HUGHES, JOHN S.; DENNIS E. LOGUE; and RICHARD J. SWEENEY. "Corporate International Diversification and Market-Assigned Measures of Risk and Diversification." *Journal of Financial and Quantitative Analysis,* November 1975, pp. 627–37.

IBBOTSON, ROGER C.; RICHARD C. CARR; and ANTHONY W. ROBINSON. "International Equity and Bond Returns." *Financial Analyst Journal,* July–August 1982, pp. 61–83. Reprinted in Donald R. Lessard, ed. *International Financial Management,* 2nd ed. New York: John Wiley & Sons, 1985, pp. 61–83.

KESTER, W. CARL. "Capital and Ownership Structure: A Comparison of United States and Japanese Manufacturing Corporations." *Financial Management,* Spring 1986, pp. 5–16.

LESSARD, DONALD R. "World, National, and Industry Factors in Equity Returns." *Journal of Finance,* May 1974, pp. 379–91.

_____. "World, Country, and Industry Relationships in Equity Returns: Implications for Risk Reduction through International Diversification." *Financial Analysts Journal,* January–February 1976, pp. 32–38.

LEVY, HIAM, and MARSHALL SARNAT. "International Diversification of Investment Portfolios." *American Economic Review,* September 1970, pp. 668–75.

REMMERS, H. LEE. "A Note on Foreign Borrowing Costs." *Journal of International Business Studies,* Fall 1980, pp. 123–34.

RUGMAN, ALAN M. "Risk Reduction by International Diversification." *Journal of International Business Studies,* Fall 1976, pp. 75–80.

SHAPIRO, ALAN C. "Financial Structure and Cost of Capital in the Multinational Corporation." *Journal of Financial and Quantitative Analysis,* June 1978, pp. 211–26.

SHAPIRO, ALAN C. "The Impact of Taxation on the Country-of-Denomination Decision for Long-Term Borrowing and Lending." *Journal of International Business Studies,* Spring/Summer 1984, pp. 15–25.

SOLNIK, BRUNO H. "Why Not Diversify Internationally Rather than Domestically?" *Financial Analysts Journal,* July/August 1974, pp. 48–54.

STANLEY, MARJORIE T. "Capital Structure and Cost of Capital for the Multinational Firm." *Journal of International Business Studies,* Spring/Summer 1981, pp. 103–20.

STAPLETON, RICHARD C., and MARTI SUBRAHMANYAM. "Market Imperfections, Capital Market Equilibrium, and Corporation Finance." *Journal of Finance,* May 1977, pp. 307–19.

STONEHILL, ARTHUR; THEO BEEKHUISEN; RICHARD WRIGHT; LEE REMMERS; NORMAN TOY; ANTONIO PARÉS; ALAN SHAPIRO; DOUGLAS EGAN; and THOMAS BATES. "Financial Goals and

Debt Ratio Determinants: A Survey of Practice in Five Countries." *Financial Management,* Autumn 1975, pp. 27–41.

STULZ, RENÉ M. "Pricing Capital Assets in an International Setting: An Introduction." *Journal of International Business Studies,* Winter 1984, pp. 55–73.

PROBLEMS

1. Blue Devil Products, Inc. Blue Devil Products of North Carolina seeks to borrow $400,000 to finance working capital needs. Blue Devil finds that it can borrow from a North Carolina bank for 10 percent per annum. Because Blue Devil has an ongoing subsidiary in Germany, it has an established credit position and so can also borrow German marks at 6 percent per annum. The marks would be exchanged for dollars at the spot rate, and dollars would later be used to acquire marks to repay the loan. Blue Devil believes that the German mark will appreciate at 4 percent per annum during the period of the loan.

Where should Blue Devil borrow?

2. Jefferson Products, Inc. Jefferson Products, Inc., a large, domestic U.S. manufacturing firm, wants to finance a $50 million expansion. Jefferson has determined that it must maintain 50 percent debt and 50 percent equity in its capital structure. Jefferson's corporate income tax rate is 50 percent.

Jefferson's New York investment banker calculates that Jefferson could raise money in the U.S. domestic market at the following costs. Both debt and equity would have to be sold in multiples of $10 million, and these cost figures show the component costs in increments of $20 million, raised half by equity and half by debt.

	Cost of Domestic Equity	Cost of Domestic Debt
Up to $20 million of new capital	12%	8%
$21–$40 million of new capital	16	12
$41–$60 million of new capital	22	16

The New York investment banker also believes Jefferson could raise new funds in London in the Eurodollar market at the following costs, also in multiples of $10 million, with the 50/50 capital structure preserved.

	Cost of Euroequity	Cost of Eurodebt
Up to $20 million of new capital	14%	6%
$21–$40 million of new capital	14	10
$41–$60 million of new capital	24	18

Each increment of cost would be influenced by the total amount of capital raised. That is, if Jefferson first borrowed $10 million in the Eurodollar market at 6 percent and matched this with an additional $10 million of equity, additional debt would cost 12 percent in the United States and 10 percent in Europe. The same relationship holds with equity.

a. Calculate the lowest weighted-average cost of capital for each increment of $20 million of new capital, where Jefferson raises an additional $10 million in the equity market and an additional $10 million in the debt market at the same time.

b. If Jefferson plans an expansion of $40 million, how should that expansion be financed? What will be the weighted-average cost of capital for the expansion?

CHAPTER SEVEN

Capital Budgeting for Foreign Projects

Capital budgeting for a foreign project uses the same theoretical discounted cash flow framework as for domestic projects. However, certain foreign complexities must be recognized and incorporated into the analysis. This can be done by modifying expected cash flows to account for specific foreign risks or, alternatively, adjusting the required rate of return. Surveys of U.S. multinational firms show that, in practice, almost an equal number of firms adjust the discount rate as modify cash flows.[1] We prefer to modify cash flows because it quantifies specific foreign risks rather than lumping them all together. Furthermore, foreign risks do not always make a project riskier than domestic projects, considering the risk-reducing benefits of diversifying investments by country and by currency. Regardless of which modification technique is used, the objective of recognizing foreign complexities is to make the analysis of foreign projects as comparable as possible to domestic projects, since they compete with each other for a share of the firm's capital investments.

FOREIGN COMPLEXITIES

The main foreign complexities are as follows.

- Rate of return from the parent's viewpoint will normally differ from the rate of return from the foreign project's view-

---

[1]The surveys in chronological order were by Stonehill and Nathanson (1968), Baker (1973), Oblak and Helm (1980), Bavishi (1981), Kelly and Philippatos (1982), and Stanley and Block (1983).

point. Explicit assumptions must be made concerning how and when funds will be returned to the parent. Cash flows accruing to the foreign project are not immediately, nor necessarily ever, available to the parent. The method chosen for repatriating the funds will determine if additional taxes must be paid, foreign exchange gains or losses incurred, and blocked funds avoided.

- Foreign projects are exposed to foreign exchange economic exposure due to unexpected changes in exchange rates. This must be considered when estimating project cash flows and repatriation of those flows.
- Political risks (such as constraints on the movement of funds or even outright expropriation of the foreign project) must be considered when estimating distant cash flows and the terminal value of the project.
- Strategic considerations are sometimes important motivations for considering foreign projects. In such cases, a foreign project's cash flows are often interrelated with cash flows originating elsewhere in the firm. For example, a foreign project's cash outflow for imports from the parent or license fees paid to the parent are cash inflows from the parent's perspective. The parent gains economies of scale, the benefits of which should be recognized in evaluating the contribution of its foreign project.

Project versus Parent Rate of Return

In analyzing a foreign project, the first step is to calculate its discounted rate of return as if it were an independent project undertaken by local investors. From the local perspective, typical cash flows would occur in local currency and would consist of an initial outflow for plant, equipment, and working capital. In subsequent years, cash inflows would consist of the project's net operating income plus depreciation. In the final year, cash inflows would consist of the project's terminal value and the recapture value of its working capital.

These local currency cash flows should be discounted back to present value, preferably using the same required rate of return that local investors would employ if the project was financed only by local equity. In this manner, the resulting net present value or internal rate of return can be compared to other local projects of similar business risk in the host country. Using an all-equity return eliminates noncomparability caused by different degrees of financial risk.

The foreign project's net present value (or internal rate of return) calculated in this manner should at least equal or exceed what a local firm could earn on the same project. Otherwise, the shareholders of the multinational firm would be better off purchasing a local firm that could undertake this project more profitably.

In some circumstances, difficulties arise in identifying a local firm capable of undertaking the project or even identifying the required rate of return from a local perspective. In such cases, the local rate of interest on host-country government bonds with a maturity equal to the maturity of the project should be used. The local government bond rate would typically incorporate expected local inflation but not the specific business risk of the project. Therefore, this rate would typically understate the required rate of return from a local perspective.

Correct measurement of expected local currency returns is important not only for capital budgeting but also because net earnings from a foreign project, translated into dollars, are typically consolidated with the parent firm's other foreign and domestic earnings. Surveys of capital budgeting practices of U.S. multinational firms confirm the importance of local currency earnings and rates of return when considering foreign projects.[2] This is consistent with corporate goals of maximizing earnings per share and return on equity, which are discussed in Chapter One.

If the foreign project passes the local-rate-of-return test, the second step is to analyze its rate of return from the parent's perspective. This depends on cash flows which can be returned to the parent. As we saw in Chapter Four, liquid funds can be returned to the parent or other affiliates in a number of ways, each of which have tax, foreign exchange, and political risk implications. The main ways to position funds are through dividends, license fees, transfer pricing on transactions with related affiliates, and loan repayments. Therefore, the capital budgeting analyst must assume what company policy will be with respect to each of these techniques. For example, what will be the size and timing of dividends and license fees? Is transfer pricing going to be a factor in moving funds? How will the project be financed, and what will be the timing and amount of loan amortization?

Since the main cash flows from the parent's perspective are financial cash flows rather than operating cash flows, calculation of the parent's rate of return will violate the normal principle that

---

[2]Ibid.

the financing decision should be considered separately from the investment decision. In the case of foreign projects, however, this is justified because funds that cannot be repatriated are not available for distribution to shareholders as dividends or to creditors for loan amortization. The parent firm's shareholders do not benefit fully from a foreign project, even if it has a high local rate of return, if local currency cannot be converted to dollars. The foreign project's value is also diminished to the parent if repatriation of funds causes additional taxes to be paid and foreign exchange losses to be incurred.

Foreign Exchange Risk

A forecast of future foreign exchange rates is necessary when analyzing a foreign project. One use is to analyze economic exposure, which must be taken into account when estimating a project's local currency cash flows. As explained in Chapter Three, an unexpected change in exchange rates can change a firm's competitiveness in both export and import markets. Unfortunately, unexpected changes are—by definition—impossible to predict. On the other hand, at the time a foreign project is being analyzed, its local currency may be undervalued or overvalued according to purchasing power parity. Recognizing inappropriately valued currencies should improve the forecast of operating cash flows for the first few years, even though the situation may be reversed in later years.

Apart from economic exposure, a forecast of future foreign exchange rates is also necessary to estimate the dollar value of funds repatriated from the foreign project. An undervalued local currency may stimulate higher local operating income, but it also reduces the dollar value of that income when funds are repatriated.

Political Risk

Political events might interfere with a foreign project's cash flows and, in severe cases, with its very existence. When facing balance of payments difficulties and pressure on its currency's value, a host country might resort to controls on conversion or transfer of its currency abroad. This results in blocked funds for the multinational firm since it has no choice but to reinvest local currency cash flows in the local country. This could lead to lost value in home currency terms, depending on the rate of return on reinvestment locally, how long the funds are blocked, and what happens to the local exchange rate.

In addition to blocked funds, political risk includes the danger of an outright expropriation of the foreign project. This causes the loss of all future cash inflows except for possible compensation from the host country. In effect, receipt of any compensation substitutes for the normal receipt of a terminal value, except compensation is normally not calculated from market value of the project. Market value would be difficult to determine in the absence of traded shares or an estimate of future cash flows free from government intervention. In some cases, governments have paid depreciated book value as compensation. In other cases, a negotiated settlement in which compensation was closer to market value was reached. In some cases, no compensation at all was paid. In such cases, the multinational firm may still receive some compensation if it has purchased political risk insurance. Such insurance is often available from a government agency of the parent firm's country when that country wants to encourage private direct investment in developing countries.

Political risk is usually introduced into capital budgeting through simulation. A foreign project's cash flows are reestimated based on various assumptions about the timing and nature of political events. The project may still have a high enough rate of return even with blocked funds or an eventual expropriation. For example, funds may be blocked temporarily, reinvested at an acceptable rate of return, and then later released for conversion. Expropriation may occur so far in the future that the required rate of return has already been earned. As a practical matter, political risk usually is only viewed as a threat to fairly distant cash flows because few firms would invest in a country that appears likely to block funds or expropriate projects in the near future.

Strategic Considerations

Investment in a foreign project may be accepted because of induced benefits to the multinational firm as a whole rather than because of the return on the project taken by itself. A foreign project may be undertaken to increase a firm's worldwide market share of an industry or product and, conversely, to deny that opportunity to its competitors. A foreign project may also import components and services from the parent, thus providing additional economies of scale and profits to the parent. Any marginal benefits or costs accruing to the multinational firm as a whole should be included in the incremental cash flows of the foreign project when calculating its rate of return.

A CAPITAL BUDGETING EXAMPLE: DAPAG

In order to illustrate some of the complexities that arise in capital budgeting for a foreign project, we will now analyze a typical example, Deutsch-Amerikanische Produktionsgesellschaft, Ag, or DAPAG for short. DAPAG has the following attributes:

- DAPAG is a wholly owned German affiliate of a U.S. parent, Ajax. DAPAG manufactures a special type of small machine tool, which sells for DM2,000 per tool. All sales are denominated in deutsche marks (DM).
- The physical volume of sales is expected to grow at 12 percent per annum for at least five years.
- The various rates of German inflation are expected to be:

    Raw material costs: +3 percent per annum
    General price level: +4 percent per annum
    DAPAG sales prices: +4 percent per annum
    German labor costs: +5 percent per annum

- U.S. inflation is expected to be 6 percent per annum.
- The weighted-average cost of capital for all equity investments of this type is 20 percent in Germany. It is also 20 percent for similar investments by Ajax in the United States.
- The value of DAPAG after the fifth year is assumed to be equal to an infinite stream of fifth-year cash flows, discounted at 20 percent.
- Production is for sale, and production volume equals sales volume; thus, there are no changes in inventory or in initial working capital.
- Components imported by DAPAG from Ajax have a direct manufacturing cost in the United States equal to 70 percent of their transfer price to DAPAG.
- A royalty fee of 4 percent of sales revenue is paid by DAPAG to Ajax. This fee is a tax-deductible expense in Germany, but it is taxable income to Ajax.
- German corporate income taxes are 50 percent. U.S. corporate income taxes are 46 percent. No carry-forward or carry-back tax credits are allowed in Germany for years in which taxable income is negative.
- In year zero, the year in which the initial investment takes place, the exchange rate is DM2.6377 per dollar. The mark is expected to appreciate relative to the dollar at 2 percent per annum. As a consequence, forecast exchange rates are:

Year 0:   2.6377
Year 1:   2.6377/1.02 = 2.5860
Year 2:   2.5860/1.02 = 2.5353
Year 3:   2.5353/1.02 = 2.4856
Year 4:   2.4856/1.02 = 2.4368
Year 5:   2.4368/1.02 = 2.3890

- DAPAG pays 85 percent of accounting profit to Ajax as an annual cash dividend. The remainder is reinvested and recaptured as part of terminal value.

Project Rate of Return from the Perspective of DAPAG

Exhibit 7.1 presents DAPAG's beginning balance sheet expressed in marks. Exhibit 7.2 shows DAPAG's accounting-based revenues and costs, also expressed in marks. Net income is shown in Exhibit 7.2, line 18, and cash dividends expressed in marks are shown on line 19.

Exhibit 7.3 shows the calculation of DAPAG's rate of return on a cash flow and all-equity basis. The format is the same used for capital budgeting for domestic projects. Interest paid by DAPAG (Exhibit 7.2, line 15) is eliminated because the weighted-average cost of capital normally includes the cost of debt. Furthermore, we are using an all-equity rate of return to evaluate DAPAG from a local perspective. Depreciation, working capital recapture, and terminal value are all added to net after-tax operating income to give net cash flows (Exhibit 7.3, line 7). These are then discounted to present value by the assumed 20 percent local (German) required rate of return after taxes.

DAPAG's cumulative positive net present value of DM3,726,000 and IRR of 22.84 percent over the five-year time horizon (Exhibit 7.3, line 10, terminal value year 5) is sufficient to justify the project from the local German perspective since it exceeds the 20 percent after-tax rate of return for an all-equity investment required by German firms to invest in a similar project.

Parent Rate of Return from the Perspective of Ajax

Although meeting the required local DM rate of return for DAPAG is important, it is even more important for Ajax to receive a dollar rate of return adequate for the risk of similar investments in the United States. Only repatriated funds denominated in dollars are totally acceptable as returns to dollar-based shareholders and creditors. Repatriation of DAPAG's DM returns to Ajax is subject to

---

EXHIBIT 7.1   Beginning Balance Sheet of DAPAG (in thousands of DM)

Net working capital ... DM10,000	Long-term debt
Net fixed assets 30,000	(12.5 percent) .... DM 8,000
	Common stock equity ... 32,000
DM40,000	DM40,000

NOTES:
1. Net fixed assets will be depreciated on a straight-line basis over six years, with no salvage value.
2. Long-term debt is denominated in DM and is an obligation of DAPAG. It is not guaranteed by Ajax. The interest rate is 12.5 percent.

---

foreign exchange risk, additional taxes, and potential political risk.

Exhibit 7.4 analyzes the value to Ajax of DAPAG's DM cash flows after repatriation of dividends and royalties. Dividends paid by DAPAG are subject to a contingent U.S. tax liability (line 5). In this case, however, credit received on German income taxes already paid in DM is greater than the U.S. tax liability (line 9). Therefore, no U.S. tax is due. Royalties paid by DAPAG are a deduction from DAPAG's income but are taxable to Ajax (line 14). Based on dividends and royalties alone, DAPAG does not pass the acceptability test from the perspective of Ajax. Cumulative net present value is a negative $907,000, and IRR is only 17.86 percent after-tax, compared to a required rate of return on similar U.S. investments of 20 percent.

Strategic Considerations in DAPAG

Exhibit 7.4 ignores returns to Ajax induced by DAPAG but not reflected in dividends and royalties from DAPAG. Ajax receives some additional returns from the 30 percent contribution margin on its exports to DAPAG as well as the opportunity to use excess foreign tax credits generated by DAPAG to shelter U.S. income tax on receipts from other foreign subsidiaries. Excess foreign tax credits can be used by U.S. firms to offset U.S. income taxes due on receipts from other subsidiaries in which the local income tax rate is lower than the U.S. tax rate. Thus, U.S. income taxes due on dividends from a subsidiary in Switzerland, where the income tax rate is low, could be offset by excess foreign tax credits in DAPAG.

Exhibit 7.5 shows how additional returns to Ajax from exports

EXHIBIT 7.2 Revenues and Costs for DAPAG, Years 1–5 (in DM)

			Year		
	1	2	3	4	5
Revenue data:					
1. Unit sales volume	25,000	28,000	31,360	35,123	39,338
2. Sales price per unit in DM	2,000	2,080	2,163	2,250	2,340
3. Total revenue (000)	DM 50,000	DM 58,240	DM 67,832	DM 79,027	DM 92,051
Variable cost per unit:					
4. German raw material	300	309	318	328	338
5. Raw material imported from U.S. parent (see details in note)	905	941	977	1,016	1,056
6. German labor	280	294	309	324	340
7. Variable cost per unit	1,485	1,544	1,604	1,668	1,734
Cost and profit data (DM 000):					
8. Total variable cost in thousands of DM (Line 1 × Line 7)	37,125	43,232	50,301	58,585	68,212
9. Gross profit (Line 3 − Line 8)	12,875	15,008	17,531	20,442	23,839
10. Royalty fee (Line 3 × 4 percent)	2,000	2,330	2,713	3,161	3,682
11. General and administrative	1,000	1,040	1,082	1,125	1,170
12. Startup costs	4,000				
13. Depreciation	5,000	5,000	5,000	5,000	5,000

14.	Earnings before interest and taxes (EBIT)	875	6,638	8,736	11,156	13,987
15.	Interest expense	1,000	1,000	1,000	1,000	1,000
16.	Pre-tax income	(125)	5,638	7,736	10,156	12,987
17.	Less German taxes @ 50 percent	0	−2,819	−3,868	−5,078	−6,493
18.	Net accounting income	(125)	2,819	3,868	5,078	6,494
19.	Cash dividends paid to Ajax @ 85 percent of accounting net income	0	DM 2,396	DM 3,288	DM 4,316	DM 5,520

NOTE: Calculation of cost of imported raw material:

	Year				
	1	2	3	4	5
Cost of imported raw material ($000)	350	371	393	417	442
Exchange rate, DM/$	2.5860	2.5353	2.4856	2.4368	2.3891
Cost of imported raw material (DM 000)	905	941	977	1,016	1,056

EXHIBIT 7.3 Project Rate of Return, All-Equity Basis, for DAPAG (DM 000)

			Year				Terminal Value
	0	1	2	3	4	5	5
1. EBIT (line 14 from Exhibit 2)		875	6,638	8,736	11,156	13,987	
2. Less German taxes @ 50 percent		437	3,319	4,368	5,578	6,993	
3. Net income, all-equity basis		438	3,319	4,368	5,578	6,994	
4. Depreciation		5,000	5,000	5,000	5,000	5,000	
5. Working capital recapture							10,000
6. PV of future income (DM6,994/.20) . .							34,970
7. Net cash flows	(40,000)	5,438	8,319	9,368	10,578	11,994	44,970
8. PV factor @ 20 percent	1.000	.833	.694	.579	.482	.402	.402
9. Present value	(40,000)	4,530	5,773	5,424	5,099	4,822	18,078
10. Cumulative net present value	(40,000)	(35,470)	(29,697)	(24,273)	(19,174)	(14,352)	3,726
11. IRR = 22.84 percent							

EXHIBIT 7.4 Value of DAPAG's Cash Flows to Ajax (DM and dollars 000)

			Year				Terminal Value
	0	1	2	3	4	5	5
1. Cash dividends from Germany (line 19 of Exhibit 7.2) in DM		0	2,396	3,288	4,316	5,520	27,600
2. Plus foreign deemed-paid tax in DM		0	2,396	3,288	4,316	5,520	27,600
3. Taxable in United States in DM (lines 1 + 2)		0	4,792	6,576	8,632	11,040	55,200
4. Exchange rate, DM/$		2.5860	2.5353	2.4856	2.4368	2.3891	2.3891
5. Taxable income in dollars (Line 3/Line 4)		0	1,890	2,646	3,542	4,621	23,105
6. Less U.S. tax @ 46 percent in dollars (Line 5 x .46)		0	869	1,217	1,629	2,126	10,628
7. Less credit for German tax paid (Line 2/Line 4) in dollars		0	945	1,323	1,771	2,310	11,552
8. Additional U.S. tax due		0	0	0	0	0	0
9. Excess foreign tax credit in dollars (Line 7 – Line 6)		0	76	106	142	184	924
10. Dividends received after tax in dollars (Line 5 – Lines 7 and 8)		0	945	1,323	1,771	2,310	11,552

EXHIBIT 7.4 *(concluded)*

	0	1	2	Year 3	4	5	Terminal Value 5
11. Royalties in DM (line 10 of Exhibit 7.2)		2,000	2,330	2,713	3,161	3,682	18,410
12. Exchange rate DM/$		2.5860	2.5353	2.4856	2.4368	2.3891	2.3891
13. Royalties in dollars (Line 11/Line 12)		773	919	1,091	1,297	1,541	7,706
14. Less U.S. tax @ 46 percent (Line 13 × .46)		−356	−423	−502	−597	−709	−3,545
15. Royalties after tax in dollars (Line 13 − Line 14)		417	496	589	700	832	4,161
16. Plus dividends in dollars (Line 10)		0	945	1,323	1,771	2,310	11,552
17. Net cash flow in dollars	(12,132)*	417	1,441	1,912	2,471	3,142	15,713
18. PV factor @ 20 percent	1.000	.833	.694	.579	.482	.402	.402
19. Present value in dollars (Line 17 × Line 18)	(12,132)	347	1,000	1,107	1,191	1,263	6,317
20. Cumulative NPV in dollars	(12,132)	(11,785)	(10,785)	(9,678)	(8,487)	(7,224)	(907)

*Original investment.

EXHIBIT 7.5 Effect of Additional Cash Flows to Ajax (DM and $000)

			Year				Terminal Value
Profits on Exports to Germany	0	1	2	3	4	5	5
1. Contribution to Ajax on exports to DAPAG in DM (30 percent × Line 5 in Exhibit 7.2)		271	282	293	305	317	1,585
2. Exchange rate, DM/$		2.5860	2.5353	2.4856	2.4368	2.3891	2.3891
3. Profit on exports in dollars (Line 1/Line 2)		105	111	118	125	133	663
4. Less U.S. tax @ 46 percent		−48	−51	−54	−58	−61	−305
5. Cash flow after tax from exports in dollars		57	60	64	67	72	358
6. Value of excess foreign tax credit in dollars		0	76	106	142	184	924
7. Additional cash flow in dollars		57	136	170	209	256	1,282
8. Original cash flow from Exhibit 7.4, line 17, in dollars	(12,132)	417	1,441	1,912	2,471	3,142	15,713
9. Revised net cash flow in dollars (lines 7 and 8)	(12,132)	474	1,557	2,082	2,687	3,398	16,995
10. PV factor @ 20 percent	1.000	.833	.694	.579	.482	.402	.402
11. Present value in dollars	(12,132)	395	1,094	1,205	1,292	1,366	6,832
12. Cumulative NPV in dollars	(12,132)	(11,737)	(10,643)	(9,438)	(8,146)	(6,780)	52
13. IRR = 20.12 percent							

and tax credits increase DAPAG's return to a positive net present value of $52,000 and an IRR of 20.12 percent. The DAPAG project would now qualify for acceptance, albeit by a small margin. Exhibit 7.5 illustrates the need to identify all incremental cash flows induced elsewhere from a foreign project. Although it is not shown in this example, the investment in DAPAG may also have some strategic consequences, such as increased economies of scale in Ajax and increased market share in Germany and worldwide. If these benefits can be quantified, which is usually a difficult task, they should be included in DAPAG's incremental cash flows.

Foreign Exchange Risk in DAPAG

In the DAPAG case, the deutsche mark is assumed to increase 2 percent per annum in value relative to the dollar. Therefore, the value of the DM cash flows exchanged into dollars in Exhibits 7.4 and 7.5 is enhanced. This appears to be a favorable foreign exchange rate development from the viewpoint of Ajax. However, it should be noted that DAPAG's assumed DM operating income might have been higher due to economic exposure if the DM/$ rate had moved the other way. In other words, DAPAG might have been more price competitive if the DM had been weaker. This depends on the development of the real DM exchange rate, considering relative rates of inflation and purchasing power parity, as described in Chapters Two and Three.

Political Risk in DAPAG

Most observers would not be concerned about political risk in Germany, with its stable, friendly government and strong balance of payments position. Nevertheless, since the DAPAG case is only designed to be illustrative, we should consider how political risk could be handled if DAPAG had been located in a riskier country.

If DAPAG's ability to pay dividends and royalties to Ajax was temporarily blocked, we would need to assume a rate of return on reinvestment in Germany. This would increase DAPAG's rate of return in Exhibits 7.2 and 7.3 but reduce Ajax's rate of return in Exhibits 7.4 and 7.5 during the period of blockage. Presumably, when the funds are unblocked, the terminal value of DAPAG from Ajax's viewpoint (Exhibits 7.4 and 7.5) would reflect the higher DM value of DAPAG caused by reinvested earnings. This might lead to a higher or lower net present value in dollar terms, depending on the rate earned by reinvestment.

If DAPAG should be expropriated, all cash inflows to Ajax

would cease, with the exception of any paid compensation. The way to handle such a crisis situation is to answer the following question: How much dollar compensation would be needed to give DAPAG a positive net present value from the viewpoint of Ajax?

For example, assume that DAPAG is expropriated at the end of year 4. By that time, Exhibit 7.5 shows that DAPAG's cumulative net present value to Ajax is a negative $8,146,000. In order to break even on this investment, Ajax would have to receive compensation at the end of year 4 with a present value of $8,146,000, using 20 percent as the discount rate. The PV factor for the end of year 4 is .482 (Exhibit 7.5). To find the undiscounted compensation amount (defined as x) for break-even, use the following formula:

$$.482x = \$8,146,000$$

$$x = \$16,900,415.$$

If Ajax receives $16,900,415 from Germany at the end of year 4 as compensation for expropriation, the DAPAG project's return would just equal the required 20 percent level.

SUMMARY

Capital budgeting analysis of a foreign project uses the same theoretical framework as for domestic projects, but several foreign complexities must be introduced.

The discounted present value of cash flows must be analyzed from the viewpoints of both the foreign project and the parent firm. Cash flows generated by the foreign project are valuable to the parent only if they can be repatriated. When funds are repatriated, foreign exchange rate changes and contingent parent-country taxes may change their value in home currency terms. At times, funds may be temporarily blocked from repatriation due to political interference by the host country. In such cases, the rate of reinvestment earned on blocked funds increases the project's return but may reduce the return to the parent, depending on the rate earned on reinvestment. If expropriation occurs, the amount and timing of compensation, if any, substitutes for terminal value as it is normally conceived in domestic capital budgeting.

When measuring cash flows for a foreign project, it is important to recognize the impact of foreign exchange economic exposure. If a foreign currency depreciates, its value to the parent will be reduced upon repatriation; but, an undervalued foreign currency may also improve the competitive position of the foreign project, thus increasing operating earnings.

Foreign projects are often motivated by strategic considerations, such as capturing market share and preempting markets from competitors as well as creating induced exports and service income for the parent or other subsidiaries. It is important to try to quantify these induced effects when measuring project cash flows.

A case example of a foreign project, DAPAG, was analyzed to illustrate the foreign complexities. Discounted cash flow returns were calculated from both the project and the parent perspectives.

ADDITIONAL READINGS

AHARONI, YAIR. *The Foreign Investment Decision Process.* Boston: Harvard Graduate School of Business Administration, Division of Research, 1966.

BAKER, JAMES C. "Capital Budgeting in West European Companies." *Issues in Financial Management* 19, no. 1 (1981), pp. 3–10.

BAVISHI, VINOD B. "Capital Budgeting Practices at Multinationals." *Management Accounting,* August 1981, pp. 32–35.

BOOTH, LAURENCE D. "Capital Budgeting Frameworks for the Multinational Corporation." *Journal of International Business Studies,* Fall 1982, pp. 113–23.

GORDON, SARA L., and FRANCIS A. LEES. "Multinational Capital Budgeting: Foreign Investment under Subsidy." *California Management Review,* Fall 1982, pp. 22–32.

HODDER, JAMES E. "Evaluation of Manufacturing Investments: A Comparison of U.S. and Japanese Practices." *Financial Management,* Spring 1986, pp. 17–24.

KELLY, MARIE E. WICKS, and GEORGE C. PHILIPPATOS. "Comparative Analysis of the Foreign Investment Evaluation Practices by U.S.-Based Manufacturing Multinational Corporations." *Journal of International Business Studies,* Winter 1982, pp. 19–42.

KIM, SUK H., and EDWARD J. FARRAGHER. "Current Capital Budgeting Practices." *Management Accounting,* June 1981, pp. 26–30.

LESSARD, DONALD R. "Evaluating International Projects: An Adjusted Present Value Approach." In *International Financial Management: Theory and Application,* ed. Donald R. Lessard. Boston: Warren, Gorham & Lamont, 1985.

OBLAK, DAVID J., and ROY J. HELM, JR. "Survey and Analysis of Capital Budgeting Methods Used by Multinationals." *Financial Management,* Winter 1980, pp. 37–41.

SHAPIRO, ALAN C. "Capital Budgeting for the Multinational Corporation." *Financial Management,* Spring 1978, pp. 7–16.

SHAPIRO, ALAN C. "International Capital Budgeting." *Midland Corporate Finance Journal,* Spring 1983, pp. 26–45.

STANLEY, MARJORIE, and STANLEY BLOCK. "An Empirical Study of Management and Financial Variables Influencing Capital Budgeting Decisions for Multinational Corporations in the 1980s." *Management International Review,* no. 3, 1983, pp. 61–71.

STONEHILL, ARTHUR, and LEONARD NATHANSON. "Capital Budgeting and the Multinational Corporation." *California Management Review,* Summer 1968, pp. 39–54.

PROBLEMS

1. Belgian Billiard Balls. The Belgian owner of a Brussels billiard ball manufacturing firm wants to manufacture in the United States to supply the American market. The investment will amount to BF20 million ($400,000 @ BF50/$), all in fixed assets, which may be depreciated over five years by the straight-line method. An additional BF5 million ($100,000) will be needed for working capital.

The Belgian entrepreneur expects to sell the U.S. subsidiary as a going concern at the end of three years for $40,000 (after all income taxes), at which time she will purchase a country villa in the Ardennes mountains in Belgium.

In evaluating the venture, the following forecasts are used:

End of Year	Unit Demand in U.S.	Unit Sales Price	Exchange Rate	Fixed Costs	Depreciation
0			BF50/$		
1	700,000	$1.00	50	$100,000	$80,000
2	900,000	1.03	48	103,000	80,000
3	1,000,000	1.06	47	106,000	80,000

Variable manufacturing costs are expected to be 50 percent of sales.

The United States imposes no restrictions on repatriation of any funds, including liquidating dividends. No new funds need to be invested in the United States for at least the first three years. The U.S. corporate tax rate is 40 percent, and the Belgian rate is 50 percent.

The Belgian entrepreneur's weighted-average cost of capital is 18 percent per annum, and her objective is to maximize her present wealth. Is the investment attractive?

2. The Flyswatter Company. The Flyswatter Company, an American firm, currently exports flyswatters to the Kingdom of Quail, earning pretax revenues of $1,000 a year. Revenue is expected to grow at 10 percent per annum for the next five years. Flyswatter's after-tax profit margin on this export revenue is 20 percent.

The government of Quail has asked that the company establish a subsidiary in Quail to manufacture flyswatters locally. The cost for capital plant and equipment would be $2,500. The plant and equipment could be depreciated on a straight-line basis over five years, at the end of which time Flyswatter will surrender all remaining assets to the Kingdom of Quail.

Sales of flyswatters in Quail are expected to increase with the proximity of a local plant, beginning in the first year at $2,200, and growing at 8 percent per annum thereafter. Costs of manufacturing will be 50 percent of sales. Of total manufacturing costs, 30 percent will be imports from the United States and 70 percent will be local labor and raw material. The Flyswatter Company will earn a pretax profit margin of 50 percent on all raw materials exported to Quail.

Corporate income taxes are 30 percent in Quail and 40 percent in the United States. The appropriate discount rate for the project is 15 percent. All profits from the subsidiary (but not depreciation) may be repatriated to the United States at the end of each year.

a. Is the project viable from a project point of view?

b. Is it viable from a parent point of view?

c. Would the analysis be different if Flyswatter found permanent reinvestment opportunities in Quail to be as profitable and no riskier than those in the United States?

3. Pinnacle Corporation. Pinnacle Corporation of the United States currently exports 24,000 tool sets per year to the People's Republic of China under an import agreement that expires in five years. Pinnacle does not expect to sell in China after the current agreement expires.

Imported sets are sold for the local currency equivalent of $40 per set. U.S. direct manufacturing costs and shipping together amount to $30 per set, and there are no other costs. The market for tool sets is constant year after year in China, neither growing nor shrinking, and is expected to continue forever. Pinnacle holds the major portion of the market.

China has no inflation, and its exchange rate with the U.S. dollar is expected to remain constant.

The government of China has suggested that Pinnacle open an assembly plant in China so that imports can be replaced with local production. The new plant would be owned and operated for five years by Pinnacle, after which the building and equipment would be sold to the government of China for net book value. At that time, working capital could be repatriated. Analysis shows the manufacturing operation would have the following financial attributes:

- *Investment outlay:* Building and equipment $ 500,000
  Working capital   500,000
  $1,000,000

- *Depreciation and investment recovery:* Building and equipment may be depreciated on a straight-line basis over five years, and funds equal to depreciation charges may be returned to the United States annually. At the end of the fifth year, the $500,000 of working capital may be repatriated to the United States.

- *Product sales price:* In return for providing protection against competing imports during the five-year period, the government of China will require all locally manufactured sets to be sold for $30 each.

- *Purchases:*

Raw material purchased from vendors in China	$10 per set sold
Components purchased from Pinnacle in the United States	5 per set sold
Total variable costs in China	$15 per set sold

The $5 transfer price for components sold by Pinnacle U.S. to its Chinese affiliate consists of $2.50 of direct costs incurred in the United States and $2.50 of pre-tax profits to Pinnacle U.S.
- *Other cash operating costs:* None.
- *Income taxes:* 50 percent rate in both the United States and China.
- *Cash flow restrictions:* No restrictions are imposed by China on the movement of funds by Pinnacle into or out of the country.
- *Discount rate for the project:* 15 percent. A table is provided below:

Year	Compound Sum	Discounted Sum	Discounted Annuity
1	1.150	0.870	0.870
2	1.322	0.756	1.626
3	1.521	0.658	2.283
4	1.749	0.572	2.855
5	2.011	0.497	3.352

Assume the investment is made at the end of year 0, and all annual operating cash flows occur at the end of years 1 through 5.

a. Given the above financial information, do you recommend that Pinnacle accept the project?

b. Pinnacle learns that if it decides against investing in China, Deep Canyon, Inc., Pinnacle's main U.S. competitor, will probably invest in China under terms similar to those offered to Pinnacle. How would this information affect your analysis and recommendation?

c. After the analysis in question *b* above, you discover the following: The investment in equipment that is included in the $500,000 of total fixed assets represents the book value of older equipment transferred to China by Pinnacle at its U.S. net book value of $100,000. The equipment could have been sold in the United States so as to realize $300,000 after all taxes and costs. New equipment, to replace that transferred to China, has already been purchased and put into operation in the United States. How would this information affect your analysis and recommendation?

d. Assume the conditions of question *b* above. China reduces its income tax rate from 50 percent to 20 percent in order to entice foreign investors to invest in that country. How would this information affect your analysis and recommendation?

e. Would your recommendation be different if Pinnacle were allowed a permanent operating presence in China, and if it expected long-run growth opportunities in that country?

f. Assume the conditions of question *b* above. Imports from the United States are paid for at once. However, China blocks all other cash remittances to the United States until the end of the fifth year, at which time all free cash may be repatriated. Funds invested in China earn 3 percent per annum, compounded annually. How would this information affect your analysis and recommendation?

g. Assume the conditions of question *f* above. However, Pinnacle is able to enter into a countertrade deal, under which it uses operating cash (depreciation and earnings) to purchase canned pickled octopus for import and sale in the United States. The supply of canned pickled octopus is unlimited, but American tastes are such that it can be sold only at 80 percent of cost. How would this opportunity affect your analysis and recommendation?

INDEX

*This book has been set on a Quadex/8400
Compugraphic phototypesetting system, in
10 and 10 point Century Schoolbook, leaded
2 points. Chapter numbers and titles are 12
point and 18 point Century Schoolbook. The
size of the type page is 27 by 47 picas.*